Untenable

Untenable

A Leader's Guide to Addressing the
Big Issues That Are Ignored, Falsely
Explained, or Inappropriately Tolerated

Gary Covert

BEP BUSINESS EXPERT PRESS

First published in 2020 by
Business Expert Press, LLC
222 East 46th Street, New York, NY 10017
www.businessexpertpress.com

ISBN-13: 978-1-94999-198-7 (paperback)
ISBN-13: 978-1-94999-199-4 (e-book)

Business Expert Press Human Resource Management and Organizational Behavior Collection

Collection ISSN: 1946-5637 (print)
Collection ISSN: 1946-5645 (electronic)

Cover and interior design by Exeter Premedia Services Private Ltd., Chennai, India

First edition: 2020

10 9 8 7 6 5 4 3 2 1

Printed in the United States of America.

Abstract

Even the best of us can find ourselves enduring situations that are negative and unsustainable. Too often, we ignore the situation or just make incremental moves. The boiling frog considers installing a ceiling fan. The deck chairs are arranged on the Titanic.

High-performing people can boost their own performance even further by developing their skills to identify and remove their untenable situations. Untenable situations are situations that are both unsustainable and that will ultimately have negative consequences. Untenable situations at best sap our creativity, vitality, and energy, at worst, they can be serious threats to our well-being or health of our organizations. This book helps identify untenable situations, describes the barriers to addressing them, and suggests novel ways to approach them.

This book is perfect for managers, leaders, and business owners who would like to be even more effective, see that effectiveness cascade into better organizational results, and would like to see their businesses grow. The book describes what untenable situations are, what they look like for leaders and organizations, and why we do not address them appropriately. The book contains useful and practical insights for leaders to help coach themselves and others to identify their untenable situations, remove barriers that may be preventing those situations from being addressed, and prevent untenable situations from occurring in the first place.

Keywords

leaders; leadership; management; managing; organizations; teams; business; organizational effectiveness; leadership skills; team effectiveness; coaching; coaching skills

Contents

Chapter 1   Untenable Situations: All Shapes, All Sizes, All Personal...1

Chapter 2   Counting the Costs..15

Chapter 3   From "What Were You Thinking?" to "Who Were You Being?" 23

Chapter 4   Asking the Wrong Questions Always Gets the Wrong Answers 31

Chapter 5   Visualize a Different State 41

Chapter 6   Not All Hurdles Are on the Outside 51

Chapter 7   Taking Steps. Break Mountains into Mole-Hills............63

Chapter 8   Discover and Rediscover Your Inner Fighter.................71

Chapter 9   Being an Inner Alchemist: Creating Novel Solutions.....85

Chapter 10   Going Public and Taking Action 97

About the Author...113
Index 115

CHAPTER 1

Untenable Situations: All Shapes, All Sizes, All Personal

- Anatomy of untenable situations
- Stuffed in the closet and swept under the rug
- Only for underperformers—*not*
- Getting real—the issue behind the issue

Untenable situations are those negative, unstainable conditions that continue to plague despite all logic. Untenable situations: what they are, why they hang around, examples in life and work and the surprising truth about who has them.

Anatomy of Untenable Situations

We all have big issues that could be handled better. Many big issues are untenable. Untenable situations are those situations that are negative or undesirable. They can show up in both life and work and frequently occur in the areas of health, finances, relationships, careers, leadership effectiveness, and organizational effectiveness. These situations are a blind spot to us or to which we have turned a blind eye.

They come in all shapes and sizes. They are hard to defend logically. They often have some element of unsustainability. They don't make sense and they are often getting worse. They are important, but for some reason, they have not been dealt with effectively to date. We often incur a lot of pain and wasted energy because of them.

Some examples:

- A business owner might be putting off a decision about quitting a business that hasn't performed in years
- An executive runs around like 13 "priorities" is normal, can be handled, and that things will be different from the results from last year
- A leader knowing that a high-level person is not working out (even the janitors know it is not working out), but no action is being taken
- A person feeling frustrated and anxious trying to perform well in a job they fundamentally do not enjoy
- A person experiencing health issues like extreme obesity or a two packs a day smoking habit
- The government reports that funds set aside for social benefits are soon to be depleted, but no politician is forthcoming with a rational plan to address
- Lack of a safety culture taken seriously by senior leaders
- Organizations that cannot deliver on promises after a big acquisition
- Organizations facing new competition with old thinking and hubris
- Organizations that cannot attract, develop, or retain exceptional talent
- An organization led by leaders with weak ethics.

A person's behavior can also be untenable. Behaviors like the ones below can lead to negative and unsustainable situations.

- Acting in a disrespectful way
- Vacillating on important decisions
- Trying to please everyone
- Impulsive decision-making
- Isolating oneself from new information or key trends
- Chronic overeating and no exercise when on the road
- Not stretching after exercise
- Looking for blame and not cause

It is important to look at untenable situations and behaviors because they represent an unsustainable condition. Just staying put or doing more of the same won't cut it. The cost of staying in the current situation has exceeded or soon will exceed the cost to address. Something needs to change and the sooner the change is made the better.

The topic of identifying and resolving negative, unsustainable issues is particularly important in the context of leadership. The demands on individuals are high and the consequences of not taking effective action in a timely manner, before opportunities are lost, are significant. This book is designed to help leaders highlight these issues clearly and smooth out any behaviors or mind-sets that are negatively impacting performance. While developed with the leader in mind, these concepts can also be used to address issues in other parts of a person's life.

So how do you know if you have an untenable situation? Basically, there are three conditions: (1) the costs of the status quo are already high or soon they will be, (2) ignoring the situation or further adaptation will not work, and (3) you care about it.

Let's take the example of a person with an unhealthy weight problem. They would likely meet all three of the criteria.
Costs of the status quo: The costs of maintaining the current weight are high and might include heart disease, diabetes, or decreased mobility.
Ignoring and adaptation will not work: Keeping the current weight or just getting bigger clothes won't help the situation.
They care about it: They personally (hopefully) care about their own quality of life and would not like to live with the consequences.

On the other hand, consider the example of a new neighborhood restaurant with a lousy offering. You might see that their service is poor and the food is not of a good value. You might also observe that the situation can't last the same way. But then again, you don't care that much because you have many other dining options and it is not your business to save. It is the restaurant owner's untenable situation, but not yours.

There are situations where further adaptation or ignoring will not fix the problem and you care about it, but the situation has not really reached a breaking point. Examples might include two direct reports who don't like each other very much, but still seem to get the job done.

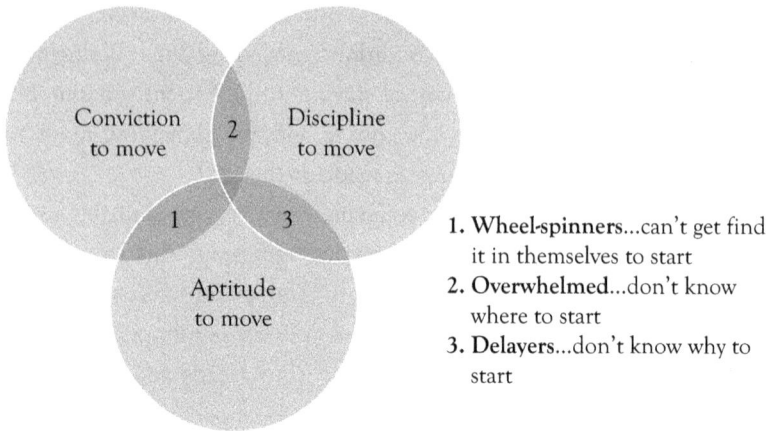

1. **Wheel-spinners**...can't get find it in themselves to start
2. **Overwhelmed**...don't know where to start
3. **Delayers**...don't know why to start

Figure 1.1 Why people stay put in their untenable situations

Can you think of some situations in your life and work that fit those three criteria? If so, this book is for you. In this book I will present strategies and tools to help correct these situations, and just as importantly, how to prevent them from occurring in the first place.

But why don't people make necessary changes when logic would tell them to do so? Why do people stay put even when the costs may be significant, the situation is worsening, and they care about resolving it positively?

As illustrated in Figure 1.1, there are three elements that must be in place for people to get moving. People must have the conviction, discipline, and aptitude to move. Let's look at each and how they interact.

Conviction to move: People must be convinced that something must be done and that things cannot continue in their current state.

Discipline to move: People have to have the inner resources to get themselves moving.

Aptitude to move: People must have the skills and knowledge of what to do to improve the condition.

A person who has conviction and aptitude but no discipline will just be *spinning their wheels* until they can find it in themselves to move. A person who has the conviction and the discipline but lacks the aptitude won't know where to start and likely will be *overwhelmed*. A person with the discipline and aptitude to move but lacks conviction will *delay* because they can't see why they should start.

Let's look again at an example of someone with a weight problem that could seriously affect their health. They would be a *wheel spinner* if they were convinced of the need to lose weight and knew the regimen they need to follow, but just can't find it in themselves to do it.

They might be stuck by being *overwhelmed* if they know they needed to lose the weight and had the discipline but did not have a plan or guidance.

They would be a *delayer* if they had a plan from a professional and had the discipline to follow it, but were not yet sold on the idea that they really did need to change.

This book will take a deeper look at each of these dimensions and offer tactics and strategies to help leaders get moving and address their situations more effectively.

Big issues may have the following additional characteristics:

- The situation may have been compartmentalized into a side issue but is soon becoming a front and center issue.
- A decision appears clear, but requires energy and fortitude to address.
- More of the same actions taken to date will not suffice.
- Explanations of why no action is being taken do not hold up to logical scrutiny.

In preparation for a scuba diving trip, I learned how to scuba dive in a pool with an instructor. In one class as we paddled around getting used to the equipment, I observed the instructor practicing taking his equipment off and then putting it back on at the bottom of the deep end of the pool. First, he took off his buoyancy device (which is a vest filled with air with the air tank mounted to it) and then he took off his mask. Lastly, he removed his regulator from his mouth. He paused, then reversed the process, and swam away. I thought it was a practical exercise and moved in to give it a try.

As with many skills, there are important nuances. The nuance of removing the air from the buoyancy device prior to removal turns out to be critical. I missed that one. Instead of ending up with all my equipment around me to put back on, the buoyancy device and air tank shot to the surface of the pool while I was stuck firmly to the bottom of the pool by the weight of my weight belt. I had held on to the air hose (and with the regulator still in my mouth) and was able to still get air. But I was in a pickle. You might call that pickle an untenable situation. I could not stay there.

That is the way untenable situations are. The cost has gotten too high to just sit there and it is time to make a move.

Stuffed in the Closet and Swept Under the Rug

One of the big reasons that untenable situations are so damaging is because of the manner in which they are often handled. They can be avoided, explained away, or compartmentalized. They are often swept under the rug or stuffed into the closet. The worst thing to do in most serious medical cases is to ignore it, but that is just what many people do with their serious situations in life. A suspicious looking mole does not benefit from being covered up. A dentist "keeping an eye" on a problematic tooth rarely changes the outcome. The situation just gets worse.

Astronomers can deduce the existence of undiscovered stars and planets by observing the movement of other known bodies in the sky. If an astronomer sees an inexplicable movement or a shadow, it may be a clue that there is something big and important out there deserving of more investigation. The same dynamics are at work for untenable situations. The effects can be felt, but the individual has not gotten to the point of focusing on what they need to do. These untenable situations are often hiding in plain sight.

Some people watch horror movies with their eyes covered or with their hands outstretched to block part of the screen. They know something is going to jump out, but try to see around it and minimize the scare. But while they may have blocked some of the screen, they still get the impact of the rest of the picture. Looking away from issues does not lessen their impact in our field of vision. They are to be completely or partially out of sight, but they are certainly not out of mind.

There are a variety of appropriate ways to handle conflict, but they are situationally dependent. Avoidance may be an excellent alternative for situations where nobody really cares about the issue, but avoidance is a lousy way to deal with issues that are important to you or others. It is not appropriate to avoid issues that are serious and likely worsening. It is a mismatch in strategy to situation.

At the time of this writing, there have been many scandals related to sexual harassment in the workplace. Many of the allegations suggest the behavior was ignored by other leaders until allegations became public and could not be ignored any more. Perhaps people involved thought that the situation would all blow over. It didn't. A strategy based on ignoring the root cause of the issue (a senior leader behaving inappropriately) perpetuated the issue and exacerbated the effects.

Sweeping under the rug or consigning to a closet are lousy strategies for untenable situations. There is only so much that can be stuffed away. There is the risk of the situation deteriorating further. We can still trip over the lumps in the carpet. A closet cluttered with the skeletons obscures things that are important or valuable.

People constantly surprise me with the amount of stuff stored in garages. In my neighborhood, I see garages that are packed to the gills with boxes. The cars are parked in the driveway exposed to the elements, but the boxes of stuff get the prime real estate. People even have periodic

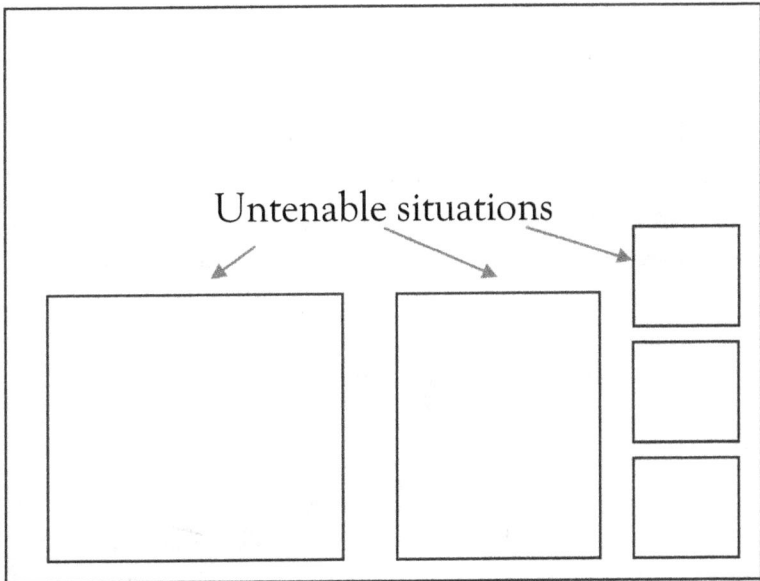

Figure 1.2 Capacity

garage sales, but dutifully pack the unsold stuff back into its place for the next sale instead of making a clean sweep.

All that stuff crowds out capacity in the garage. People also need capacity to handle big and important things. We can have one big issue the size of a car or a big moving box that is diminishing our capacity. We can also have lots of little issues that are the size of a Chinese food take-out boxes that taken together take up a lot of space. As can be seen in Figure 1.2, all that clutter crowds out good capacity. People have unlimited creativity but finite energy. Getting rid of these issues improves conditions but another key benefit is expanded capacity to handle other things.

As one of my wise clients likes to observe, "hope is not a strategy." Yet many seem to be caught in a loop of sweep and hope and hope and sweep. We can all understand the inappropriateness of the proverbial head in the sand. At some point even the ostrich has to wonder about its reputation.

Recently, de-cluttering and organizing stuff in the house has gotten very popular. So much so that donation centers have seen huge spikes in donations. It seems like people can feel good with less. Maybe you are ready to clean out and make some room too.

Only for Underperformers—Not

As surprising as it is that undesirable situations exist despite all logic and cost, it is just as surprising to consider who has them. While we may be tempted to think that only underperformers would be troubled by untenable situations, the truth is many high performers have them too. Having untenable situations is no badge of honor, but many people succeed despite operating under the weight of unsustainable conditions.

I have seen leaders trying work effectively while taking on all the primary care responsibilities for a loved one with no adjustments at work. I have seen leaders wearing themselves out without any delegation to willing and able staff. I have seen leaders doing the job of underperforming direct reports.

I have seen people with huge amounts of responsibility for people, production, and profits be stymied by situations that cannot go on anymore. These people are extremely bright and driven. Unfortunately, neither of those qualities are sure to prevent these kinds of situations. CEOs can have these kinds of issues. VPs can have these kinds of issues. Successful business owners can have these kinds of issues. Successful people can be blind to some realities too.

Many high performers would achieve even more plus materially boost their enjoyment if they were to take appropriate action to improve their own big issues.

Just as people might be surprised that successful people have these problems too, successful people may have trouble wrapping their head around the fact that they have issues weighing them down. Marshall Goldsmith (a well-known executive coach and author of *What Got You Here Won't Get You There*) has observed that successful people are often superstitious about change. If they are enjoying great success (his thinking goes), then any deviation may derail that success. Goldsmith's adage of "what got you here won't get you there" then applies in the sense that some people might not want to change or not understand why they should change.

People from all walks of life in all levels of success and responsibility have untenable situations. We can all gain by addressing untenable situations. Work performance can improve. We can move faster. We can dedicate efforts to the highest and best priorities.

The most impressive looking ship in the ocean may still have barnacles on the hull, slowing down the ship and killing efficiency. Just a few pounds of missing pressure in a bicycle tire slows down even the most high-tech racing bike. Imagine a race car trying to compete in a drag race with its chute deployed from the starting line. Just like everyone has some sort of personal struggle or loss that is not worn overtly like a t-shirt (such as dealing with difficult family situations, death, or disease), successful people have their fair share of tough situations that they are ignoring or are trying to gut out, just like anyone else.

Getting Real: Importance and Causes

It is important to note that negative situations can range in degrees of seriousness. As can be seen in Figure 1.3, the importance of negative issues can run the gamut from the innocuous (like a crummy car for a teenager), to the merely irritating (like poor customer service from government agencies), to the distracting (like a computer that keeps crashing), to the intolerable (like senior leaders behaving unethically). The degree to which the situation is unsustainable should inform the degree to which we assertively address it. For many people dealing with an untenable situation, the utility of avoidance and adaptation have run their course and it is time to get more serious.

The problem occurs when people are not taking active approaches to serious or intolerable conditions. Serious conditions require serious action. And too often even the best of us have deluded ourselves about the seriousness of the situation and about the effectiveness of our response.

Serious conditions require effective responses. Those that have seriousness situations and timid responses are like the ostrich—ignoring and hoping. We need to be more like beavers, who will literally change the landscape to redirect things in a way that best work for us.

And we do not want to dilute our energies by focusing on those things that are merely irritating or innocuous when we have big issues that are intolerable (or soon will be) right in front of us.

In addition to getting real about the seriousness of the situations and about our efforts to date, we need to get real about *causes*.

If the cause of the situation is fuzzy, or is covered in a justification, it will be difficult if not impossible to improve the condition. Sometimes what people say is the issue may not be the real issue and does not stand up to scrutiny.

People will say their schedules are crazy busy because of the demands of the job, but sometimes the issue is they just frankly that they like being

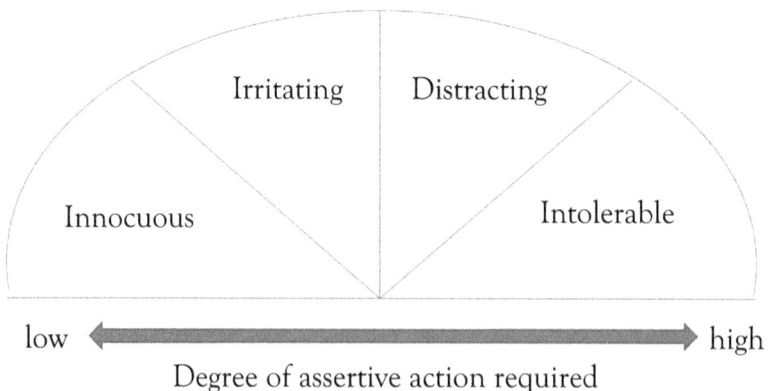

Figure 1.3 Degrees of unsustainability

busy. They get some level of satisfaction from being needed. The reason might be the person does not feel comfortable to say "no" or they want to be liked.

People might say that talent is hard to find, but the cause may be that the organization has gotten a poor reputation as an employer due to how they have treated people who subsequently left.

People might want to maintain the facade at their apparent reason or just haven't come to grips with the real reason. Sometimes the real issue is something they are fully aware of, but don't want to say.

A business owner whose business was suffering because of a poor performer in a key position said he has no choice but to keep them because "there is no talent around here." The truth was he was just scared of the possible repercussions of firing someone and being seen as the bad guy.

Or a business owner postpones a decision to exit a clearly underperforming business until they get yet more information. The real reason for the delay is he does not want to look like a quitter. He already has all the information he needs but does not want to admit defeat.

Career decisions can have issues behind issues. I have seen people stick with a job saying that they just need to have a better attitude when the real point of dissatisfaction was the pay. They explained it away because they did not want to be seen (or see themselves) as somebody who "just cares about the money."

A great number of people stay too long in jobs they do not like with the explanation that they do not have enough experience for a new career. The real reason is that they are scared to move and have high security needs.

Too often there is some fuzzy logic being applied. We need to peel the onion and get to the root of the issue. Often, at the core of the issue there is fear of the unknown, fear of what others will think, or fear of not looking consistent. Only when we get to the root of the issue can we make significant progress.

It might take some pick and shovel work to get to uncover the real issues, but it is worth it. Illogic (excuses and weak rationale) makes for squishy ground and one cannot build or pivot on squishy ground. We need to get to higher ground. Rational ground.

Exercise

Let's consider an undesirable condition (or conditions) in your life and work.

What big issues or challenges would you like to see dramatically improved? To assist in your thought process, consider rating your degrees of satisfaction for each of the following:

- Leadership/personal effectiveness
- Team/organizational effectiveness
- Career
- Work–life balance
- Health/fitness
- Relationships
- Other
- Why has the issue not been resolved? Analyze the situation in relationship to your conviction to change, discipline to change, and aptitude to change.
- How serious is the situation? Has it progressed to other areas, distracting, or intolerable? What has been your degree of effort to resolve? How do they compare?
- What do you feel is the real, honest root of the problem?
- Do you care about the resolution of this issue?

The first step to resolving issues is to clearly identify the issue. Take the time to highlight some issues that you would like to see materially different. The rest of this book will look at techniques to help resolve those issues and prevent them from recurring.

Summary and Tips

- *Leaders and organizations may have performance that is hampered by not addressing issues that are negative and unsustainable.*
- *Situations can be untenable and behaviors can also be untenable.*
- *The reason people and organizations do not take effective action is because of three factors; lack of conviction, lack of aptitude,*

or lack of discipline. All three must be in place in order to take effective action to resolve an undesirable situation.

- *People from all walks of life (including very successful people) may have some serious challenges that they have not addressed appropriately to date.*

CHAPTER 2

Counting the Costs

- Dragging that horse around
- Is the juice worth being squeezed?
- Collateral damage
- An inside hit job

There are a variety of costs related to untenable situations. Some are overt and some covert. Addressing untenable situations requires a conviction of the need to change and a frank reckoning of the costs of the status quo. Costs include the obvious like opportunities to the not-so-obvious like self-esteem.

Dragging That Horse Around

Business people are familiar with the concept of carrying costs. They arise from costs related to holding onto inventory or storing goods. A store might want to sell a thousand tires in a month, but there is a cost associated with storing them in the meantime. The tires must be stored, and perhaps financed. Carrying costs are real money to businesses. Untenable situations also have a carrying cost. There is a cost to dragging that proverbial horse around and it can extract a serious toll.

Not addressing untenable situations puts a lot of energy into the system for no good purpose. People worry, agonize, ruminate, and otherwise spend energy while staying in place.

Personal trainers will tell you there is no excuse for not working out, even when on the road. The reason is because people can get a great workout with no equipment and in a little space by just using body weight resistance, using a jump rope, or even jogging in place.

That's a great news for road warriors that want to stay in shape, but too many people apply the same concept to their untenable situation.

They spend a ton of effort in place for no good reason. They work up a sweat but get nowhere. You might think of carrying costs as the effect of being on an emotional hamster wheel.

The mere fact of having the untenable situation extracts a price. The simple fact that the unwanted situation is still there and yet to be unresolved consumes thought capacity and emotional reserves.

Simply having the thing in the room consumes energy and unnecessarily pollutes our personal space. In winter, there are many warnings for people to not bring outside heaters inside for additional heat. The danger comes from poor ventilation and carbon monoxide. It can be deadly. And yet, people keep situations around that metaphorically pollute their environment and endanger their mental and emotional health.

We know that the horse is dead and that we should stop kicking it, yet somehow we have decided that it makes sense to shoulder that enormous carcass around so we can kick it some more later. It's as if people have forgotten what dead horses are really good for: fertilizer. They do, in fact, make awful backpacks.

Is the Juice Worth the Squeeze?

In addition to the emotional "carrying costs" described above, unresolved issues also have other direct costs. These costs can be tangible or intangible. Direct costs are costs that can be tied directly to not taking action. These can include time, money, and energy spent.

There are also opportunity costs. These are the benefits that are not enjoyed because a situation was not improved. Once a person renovates a house, they can enjoy the utility of a nicer kitchen or an upgraded swimming pool. The homeowner gains utility from making the improvement. The longer that action is deferred, however, the farther out the benefits are delayed and utility is lost. A person might also lose out on opportunities that may never come again. A door was closed because action was not taken.

In the context of a career, costs might include:
- Low enjoyment in the work today
- Income that is below potential
- Frustration from not utilizing strengths

- Underperformance in the current role
- Lack of development of skills for new roles
- Enjoyment derived from a future role

In the context of health, costs might include:
- Diminished quality of life
- Reduced ability to go new places or experience new things
- Reduced time with family and friends
- Unnecessary pain and suffering
- Reduction in the ability to enjoy old hobbies and activities
- Social isolation

In an organizational context, costs might include:
- Disempowered people not executing
- Ongoing operational inefficiencies
- Lost team effectiveness
- Diminished personal effectiveness
- Key talent losses
- Reduced competitiveness
- Strained partnerships
- Diminished innovation
- Squandered capital
- Market share
- Unhappy shareholders
- Tarnished reputation

These costs can add up and it usually does not take an accountant to figure it out. With a little consideration, these costs become apparent and are usually quite substantial.

Collateral Damage

If a situation is not good for you, it is likely not good for others. We should also consider collateral damage.

One small business owner I knew took the position that he could successfully grow his business by delegating everything to an office manager.

(This is the fantasy of many professional business owners like dentists.) Of course, the business did not grow and he certainly suffered financial costs for his decisions, but others suffered too. His staff got salaries, but no raises or bonuses. The community did not benefit from expanded or improved services. The office manager was insecure so no new talent was attracted and high achievers did not stay. Those were just the tangible collateral impacts.

There was also emotional collateral impact on the people around him. The owner would get frustrated and would vacillate between withdrawal and jumping back in to regain control. Those around him suffered because he would lash out when his patience was lost. One can only imagine what it was like at home.

Another business owner kept avoiding financial reality and paid partner-level wages to people who were actually performing as subcontractors. At a point in time, the owner could tolerate the situation, but as time passed, the business could no longer support it. When he finally brought it up to the partners, it was a big deal. The individuals had to take a large financial hit late in their careers and hard feelings were shared all around.

Unfortunately, not effectively handling issues can impact those around us that love and care for us the most. These people can bear the brunt of misplaced frustration in the form of reactions that can swing from sullen silences to sudden expressions of anger. Add pressure to any system and it will be contained until it hits a weak point. If relief valves are not used or pressure dealt with appropriately, the pressure will be released inappropriately.

An Inside Hit Job

So far, we have identified four kinds of costs: carrying costs, direct costs, opportunity costs, and collateral costs. There is one more type of cost that is worth exploring and it has to do with self-esteem.

Think of the times where you have taken some proactive, perhaps overdue, action. A car is in need of overdue service, a garage needs to be cleaned out, or a form needs to be filed. When these tasks are done, there is usually a very positive feeling of accomplishment or control.

Conversely, not dealing with a situation prolongs negative feelings. People feel like they are at the mercy of situations. People may feel that they are not being authentic. People may feel they are not being their best. All of these can negatively impact self-esteem.

One leader I knew had contorted himself to try and fit into a position he did not and could not really enjoy. He enjoys creating new approaches in business and thrives in situations with a high degree of latitude. His employer was very traditional and his creativity and unconventional thinking were not highly valued. Trying to fit himself in that box was denying the obvious truth. When his employer was not pleased, he felt it must be his fault. He started to doubt his worth and felt he was not being genuine to who he really was.

Other leaders I have seen have become masters at avoiding important conversations. While the outward costs are obvious (like lack of organizational effectiveness and hard feelings), the inside costs include feeling like they are not a standup person. Avoiding measures become great ammunition for a person's inner critic.

Not taking steps to address the untenable situation also reinforces the idea that there are few choices. By letting these things fester, it's like letting the fox into the hen house. And the chickens getting taken out one by one include confidence, self-esteem, feelings of authenticity, and feelings of control.

On benefits...

While I have spent time on the costs, there are certain benefits to not doing anything. If there were no benefits at all, the situation may have already been resolved, right? Maybe there really were some "benefits" to not taking appropriate action to date. It is ok to have good reasons, but we just need to beware that they are not simply justifications.

Here are a few "benefits" that can actually be quite harmful:

A Desire to Appear Consistent. People like to stay consistent. People have an aversion to looking wishy-washy. A change of direction even in light of new information can be difficult for people. If the desire to appear consistent is keeping a person from looking at new information this can be a big problem.

A Desire to Avoid Hard Work. The human brain is very lazy. It does not like to expend energy without need. Hence all the short-cuts in thinking: dogma, biases, presumptions, etc. Likewise, a person may just see taking the issue on as really just too much right now. Sometimes it may be true. Sometimes it is just a pretense and is, in fact, laziness.

The Desire to Preserve an Identity. There may be benefits to inaction, because a current identity (as a leader or as a member of a certain group) might suffer or comes with some advantages like sympathy.

A Desire to Preserve Relationships. Sometimes the actions required will put current relationships at risk and raises issues of fear, loss, or guilt.

A Desire to Avoid Uncertainty. The fear of the unknown can paralyze. The current condition may be awful, but the devil we know may be more attractive than the one we don't.

A Desire to Avoid Blame. Taking no action will often give people the cover they need to avoid being blamed. Doing nothing gives them a sense of plausible deniability.

We need to be wary of short-term "benefits" that are in fact pretenses to not taking appropriate action. These can get in the way of effectively addressing issues and thereby continuing to suffer the costs and miss out on real benefits. Real benefits are those benefits derived from an improved condition. Benefits that are mere pretenses are empty calories and not worth chewing on.

Get Real Math: Add 'em Up

It's time for some "get real" math. Now that we have highlighted some of the categories of costs, let's get yours out in the open. Use the list below to help add up the costs that may be accruing to not taking action on a situation that may need more attention from you.

- What is it costing you to continue to carry this unresolved issue (e.g., the emotional costs of worry, anxiety, rumination or distraction)?
- What are some of the direct costs related to not resolving the issue (e.g., time, money, energy)?
- What opportunities have been lost or might be lost by not resolving the issue?

- Have there been collateral costs? Have others also been adversely affected or might in the future?
- What has been the impact on your self-esteem?
- To what degree has lack of effective resolution to date been impacted by some perceived "benefits" to inaction (e.g., desire to appear consistent, desire to preserve identity or relationships, desire to avoid uncertainty, or desire to avoid possible blame)?

It's important to surface the costs of the status quo. Having a full accounting of the costs can help people break the cycle and take some action. The point at which the cost of staying exceeds the cost of movement is an excellent time to move. By surfacing these costs, we can start to infuse rationality into a situation that is likely starved for it.

At one point, the Titanic was habitable. In another moment, it was not. At one point, the frog was taking a bath. At another point, he was becoming soup. Not all unseen costs will reach a catastrophic level. But they can grow enough where all logic would point to the benefits of resolution of the problem and not still more resolution of spirit.

Summary and Tips

- Get real on all the costs of not taking effective action. Costs include tangible costs like money, time, and energy related to direct costs and opportunity costs. Unresolved issues can also exact an emotional cost like worry, anxiety, rumination, and fear. I call these carrying costs.
- Do not forget to account for potential hits to self-esteem and for collateral damage.
- Be wary of poor excuses masquerading as benefits to inaction.
- Calculating the costs is no guarantee to force productive action, but it is a powerful step to put more logic into the system and strip away the pretenses.

CHAPTER 3

From "What Were You Thinking?" to "Who Were You Being?"

- What lies beneath
- Good wolves, bad wolves, and their cousins
- Symptoms, sources, and solutions
- Pro forma thinking

Untenable situations can have an ontological dimension. Who we are being has enormous influence and can create untenable situations and allow them to continue. Who we are being in a given situation can be both the source and solution to our problems.

What Lies Beneath

Even coaches get coached. Once I was complaining to a mentor coach about some situation of mine that had gone south. His question caught me off guard: *Who were you being that allowed that to happen?*

While we can explain or rationalize things from here to eternity, the genesis of thinking comes from who we are being in any particular moment. If we are scared, our thinking, our solutions, and our approaches will come from a place of fear and likely will have diminished quality. If we are being confident, our thinking, our solutions, and our approaches will come from a place of confidence and will likely be at a higher quality.

I often see the phenomenon of being "overly deferential" with emerging leaders in organizations. They overthink the importance of hierarchy. Consequently, they are too submissive and their ideas lack punch and

Being ———→ Thinking ———→ Action ⟨ High impact / Diminished impact

Figure 3.1 *Quality of Being on the Quality of Impact*

clarity. By being too deferential, they trade away IQ points and reduce their ability to influence senior leaders.

As illustrated in Figure 3.1, the quality of who a person is being at a particular time has a direct impact on the quality of the actions they produce.

In sales, it is said that the first sale is to yourself. If a person is coming from a state of being "internally unsold," then their entire thought process changes. They think about tactics to manipulate or corral people into a decision. Their approach comes across as clumsy and contrived. But an "internally sold" person's enthusiasm shines through. Being internally sold trumps nearly any complicated sales tactic. Attempting an assumptive close ("so shall I get the paperwork ready?") without enthusiasm and authenticity will likely just come across as clunky.

Who we are being can distort reality and cloud thinking. A business owner, with decades of experience, considered himself an authority on success. However, the reality was that his clientele was drying up, his business systems were slipshod, and his staff could care less. There were concrete things he could do to change his conditions, but he never did. Being "a successful business owner" hijacked his thinking and would not allow him accept that he had made some poor decisions. He rejected suggestions and justified not changing his approach because *that's what he had done successfully to date.* He was being defensive and an "authority on success," even though it was clear he was on the wrong path.

Being drives thinking and it can either improve performance or degrade it.

Good Wolves, Bad Wolves, and Their Cousins

There is a story about a good wolf and a bad wolf living inside each person. The good wolf is the brave part of oneself. The bad wolf is the fearful side of ourselves. The two wolves are said to be constantly at war with one another. The question for people is which one we will let win. Fear and courage are two fundamental states of being and can greatly impact effectiveness.

Fear is a common source of untenable situations. People are scared to assert themselves. They're scared to speak up. They're scared of potential consequences. They're scared of looking foolish. By being scared, we can evaluate the situation incorrectly. The plans made to address the dire situations may be faulty. The logic used to explain the situation may be misguided.

A leader I worked with allowed himself to be intimidated by his staff. As a management practice, he said he corrected poor behavior of individuals by addressing the entire group about the need to follow some policy. He did this instead of addressing the problem directly with that one person who was not following the policy. His justification of the approach was that he did not want to make the individual feel bad. In truth, he did not want to make himself feel bad. So he came up with a convoluted argument and a lousy response. He was being scared of what his direct reports thought, and it guided him to choose poor actions.

Being courageous, on the other hand, can improve many situations. Courage can keep people on the right track. Courage can unlock creativity. From my perspective, it takes a lot of courage to be a successful stand-up comedian. They are the only one on stage. People will either laugh or they won't. The material can be gold or be a dud. Yet they get up there and take the applause and the potential hits to the ego. Being courageous allows them to try new things, be distinctive, and get back in

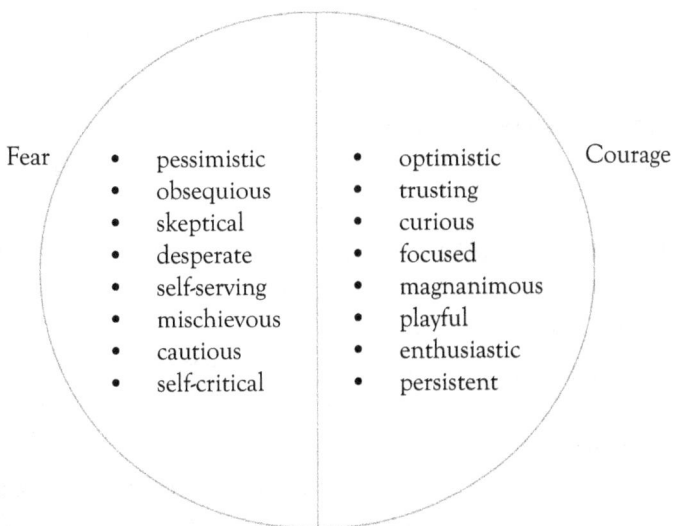

Figure 3.2 *Fear, courage, and some of their close cousins*

there when things don't go well the first time. Courageous journalists ask the tough questions and do not take the easy answers. Courageous leaders question the assumptions of their organization and their industry; they resist thinking like the herd even when it is unpopular.

While the two "wolves" of fear and courage represent two big states of being, there have some close cousins. Figure 3.2 highlights some of the near relatives. One can be pessimistic or optimistic. One could be skeptical or trusting. One can be cautious or confident.

Each state of being can color how we approach a situation. A very confident person may see opportunities. A person being very skeptical might miss real opportunity by focusing too much on risk. A person being very desperate might take a job way too small for them or not otherwise a good fit. They may evaluate the landscape of career opportunities incorrectly. They may overlook their own genuine strengths that might actually be highly valued in the market.

We can improve our outcomes dramatically if we can shift more of our time "being" on the courage side of the equation. How much of your time do you spend on the fear side? How much of your day do you spend on the courage side? Why is that? What if we could make a dramatic shift to even more courage? I think we would see much faster resolution of issues. I think we would also see many negative issues being prevented from occurring in the first place.

Some states of being might include an *assumed role* like the patriarch, the steady one, the loyal one, the dependable one, the good child, or the friend. Sometimes the role is appropriate to the situation and sometimes not. Sometimes the role was right at the beginning, but circumstances have changed and the role no longer fits.

For example, some leaders fall into the trap of trying to play the friend role. This is especially common when a person gets promoted from within their peers. Trying to be the friend and be the supervisor causes many problems including eroding effective enforcing and causing hard feelings with team members who feel excluded.

In families sometimes, one spouse feels they must take the role of enforcer, while the other spouse gets to be the good guy. This arrangement can allow a child to play one parent against the other. The spouse who is forced into an enforcer role may also carry some resentment.

Look at the list below. As you review, consider if any of the states of being may be potential source or solution for some issues you want to address more effectively.

Roles of Being

- Being the enforcer
- Being the responsible one
- Being the friend
- Being the boss
- An owner
- A direct report
- An employee
- A pencil pusher
- The expert
- The successful one
- The older/younger sibling
- The hero
- The imposter
- The patriarch/matriarch
- The nurturer
- The perfectionist
- The fixer
- The "go to" person

Roles provide a framework for how we think and behave. Roles can have limiting effects or they can have expansive effects. We can take on frameworks that are too small like thinking of ourselves as "just" middle managers. (Actually, the qualifier of "just" should be a red flag unless being used with self-deprecating humor or irony, like a person saying they are "just" a simple businessperson when they have a distinctive track record of success.) We can also consider relabeling a role to better fit the bigger impact we want to have.

Reflection

What are some of the roles you have defined for yourself? Which ones do you find to be beneficial to you? Are there some roles that don't seem to work anymore? What impact has role selection had on some of your big issues? Are there different ways you can re-frame roles that are outdated and no longer beneficial?

Symptoms, Sources, and Shifts

We can raise effectiveness by observing symptoms of a problem, determining potential sources that might come from who we were being at that moment, and then consider some solutions.

For example, a leader might say "people think I am wishy-washy." That is their symptom. The source might be "being a people pleaser." The solution might be to think of themselves as a solution-seeker.

A leader described to me once feeling like he was "stretched like a piece of taffy." I think many leaders have experienced this feeling. For many, it is because they are trying to be "the helpful one." While there are many tactics to choose from (like just saying no, or being more stringent about calendar space), real progress might be made by shifting from being "the helpful one" to another type of being like the "ridiculous productive one."

Another leader described feeling like he was just going in circles trying to get consensus from all the other groups in an organization. He said that he felt his role was to "be the liaison," which to me, sounded like simply being a messenger and not the leader he was being paid to be. He shifted his thinking to "be the advocate" which let him see a better and less labor intensive way to move things forward.

A leader who often surprises his team with his fast and unilateral decisions, might be jumping in because he is convinced he is needed to "the fixer" because nobody else seemed prepared to make the decision. The leader might benefit from being the "focuser" and making sure that people came to a decision on priority items.

Table 3.1 Moving from Symptoms to Shifts

Symptoms	Sources	Shifts
People say leader is too demanding	Being the perfectionist	Pragmatic innovator
Team surprised with fast and unilateral decisions	Leader feeling need to be "the fixer" because nobody taking actions	Priority focuser
Team members feel there are favorites	Supervisor trying to be the friend	The understanding leader

Once a person has looked at who they were they may have been that may have caused the problem, they can then look at possible new ways of being. These new ways of being do not need to be a 180 degree change from the state of being that they were being in prior. Slight shifts and nuances can still be effective. It can be like shifting to a better grip on a large or awkward piece of furniture we are trying to move. A shift to a better grip can make all the difference.

As Table 3.1 illustrates, we need to look at the symptoms, identify the source, and consider some possible beneficial shifts.

Beware the slingshot effect and overcompensating. A person might be tempted to say they were optimistic so now they need to be skeptical. Not true. Perhaps they need optimism. In fact, the state of being may be a blend of two traits. If a person were being naive or too trusting then bouncing to skeptical won't help. But being a *verifying truster* may be more useful.

Pro Forma Thinking

Pro forma financial statements are statements about future financial conditions. They paint a picture of what performance will look like in the future. We can also make pro forma statements about how we want to be in a future situation.

Deciding how we want to be in advance is a lot better than winging it. A speech can go sideways quickly if we wing it. Under pressure, we do not rise but sink to our level of experience. We can also sink to a default state of being.

Some people have a strong preference to be deferential, or to be cautious, or to be bold. Those are admirable states but not always what the doctor ordered for a given situation. My dog, Candy, has a default inclination to submission. Her submissiveness is endearing and probably one of those survival traits that kept her ancestors close to the camp fire. But it is her one and only defensive card. When she was attacked by another dog (who would have killed her if not stopped), she could only go to her submission state. For some humans, they are a one-trick pony of being "nice" in any given situation.

The state a person chooses has to fit the situation at hand. For example, a person should not try to be the accommodator if the situation cannot be accommodated to. A person should not try to be the fixer if it is not their problem to fix. A person cannot be the hero if the other person does not want or need saving.

So take the ontological view and do some historical reconnaissance. Who were you being at the time the situation developed? Who have you been during the situation? To what extent has your state of being helped or hindered the situation? What are some possible new states that are worth trying on?

If being colors thinking, that it is critical to get the foundational parts sorted out. Thinking better is essential, but that can be a band-aid if who we are being has not been addressed. The labels we paste on ourselves make a big impact on how and what we think, how we behave, and how we analyze situations.

Exercise

Consider current and past situations in which you did not accomplish the results you wanted.

- What were some of the behavioral symptoms you saw during that situation?
- To what extent did fear/courage and assumed roles contribute to the situation occurring and preventing effective resolution?
- What modifications can you make?

Summary and Tips

- Realize that states of being can enhance or degrade execution of behaviors, tactics, and strategies.
- Responsibly diagnose potential remedies with "who was I being that allowed that to happen?"
- Consider blending different states of being.
- Avoid oversteering and just "trying to be the opposite."
- Be aware of inappropriate roles for a situation and roles that may be outdated.
- Decide in advance how you would like to be. Check in from time to time and see if your aspirational state matched the real state.

CHAPTER 4

Asking the Wrong Questions Always Gets the Wrong Answers

- Yes, there are dumb questions
- Now you're talkin'
- The high art of impossibility thinking
- Augmented intelligence: Getting outside help

Asking the right questions is essential to correctly diagnose situations and to move forward effectively. This chapter describes examples of great questions and a sequence to move forward that helps break out of circular logic and defeatist traps.

Yes, There Are Dumb Questions

Questions are powerful. They get us to stop and think. They can motivate us to consider new paths or options, but some questions are clearly more powerful than others. Questions should improve effectiveness, not degrade it. It is not just a matter of asking questions, it is a matter of asking good questions.

One can tell good questions from bad ones by looking at the degree to which they raise awareness and help forward the action. One can see this dynamic illustrated in Figure 4.1. If the question (or line of questioning) can do both, you have a home run. As we discussed in Chapter 3, *who are you being that allowed that to happen?* was a home run question for me. It got me thinking about my ineffective mind-set and also what I might do differently. A less useful question might have been

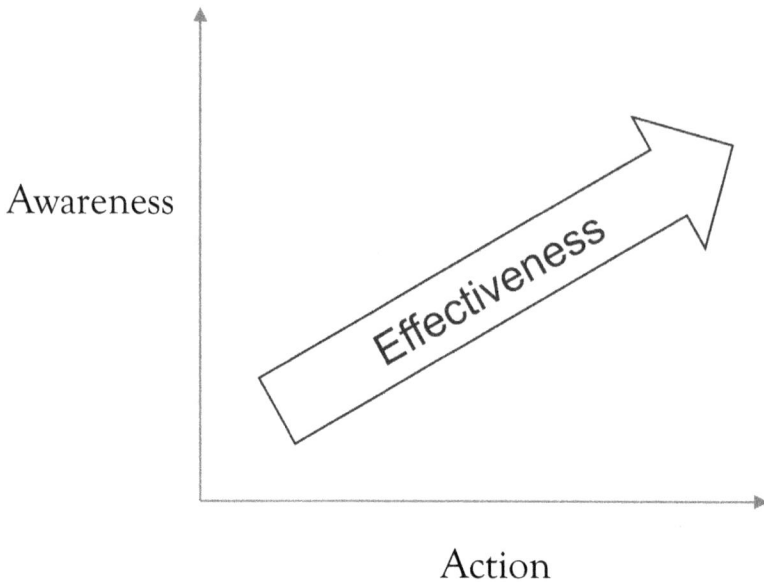

Figure 4.1 Awareness and Action

"what was your business partner thinking?" My awareness may have gone up, but I suspect that would have taken less effective action because my responsibility would not have been in the picture. The question is interesting, but would not really get me anywhere.

Likewise "Why don't you do X?" would not have helped me much because my awareness would stay low even if I made some forward motion or action. What is best to have is a situationally enhanced awareness that drives action.

Useful questions drive awareness of things like:

- What people want to accomplish (objectives)
- Assumptions
- Options
- Any lessons or learning to date
- The bigger picture
- Strengths that can be used
- Opportunities that could be exploited
- Other considerations

Great questions for action will:

- Define next steps
- Set time frames
- Enable accountability

Some questions are bad because they do a poor job of raising aware-ness and forwarding action. Some questions are bad because of poor *premises*. The questions are poor because the starting point is off. Below are some questions I have encountered that were poor because of their basic premise.

- How can I give him negative feedback indirectly? (*Wouldn't direct feedback be better?*)
- Why don't my colleagues understand this is a policy we all agreed to? (*Is this really something they believe they agreed to?*)
- How do I best run the business without me? (*Many things can be delegated, but ownership and leadership are not among them.*)
- How do I work with people that are clearly not as smart as me? (*What makes you think they are not smart?*)
- What team building should I do to get my team to trust me again? (*What did you do to lose trust? Is team building going to fix that?*)
- How do I get better at delivering presentations to buyers? (*Are you really talking to buyers in those meetings and why are you hiding behind presentations and not getting better at relating with senior decision makers?*)
- Where should I travel after I retire? (*What is stopping you now and why on earth would you wait?*)
- What more can I do to follow-up on action items of my people? (*Don't they have primary responsibility on how to keep you updated?*)
- What would my father/mother/family/friends think? (*Are you working to simply please them or can you also please yourself?*)

There is a popular TV show in which a dermatologist surgically removes growths and blemishes from patients. Many of these patients have these blemishes and growths on their faces, necks, or hands and have tried to get by with covering them up or avoiding social contact. The show centers around the doctor "popping" these growths. With a scalpel and within a few minutes, most of these people get immediate relief from pain and any feelings of embarrassment. We too need to be surgical about popping our premises and the premises of others.

Interviews with CEOs of major companies are often good examples of premise busting. They are very careful to not readily accept the premise of an interviewer's question. (This is different from what you will often see with politicians, which is often just simple evasion.) They will point out that the line of questioning is not highlighting the most important points or misses some key facts.

We need to be aware of our premises. People can miss a faulty premise for a few reasons:

- *Momentum: The team or organization seems to be far down the trail of an initiative and people think it may be too late to bring things up.*
- *Assumption that it has been covered: People think that someone must have considered the point already.*
- *Belief that it is not our place: People might think that it is not their role to bring something up.*
- *Busy: People get too busy and the important points tend to become a blur and not brought up or considered.*

There are three basic requirements to be an excellent premise popper: sensitivity, good questions, and flexibility. First, we need to be sensitive to premises. We need to be aware that positions are built on assumptions of facts and conditions. Are there really no jobs around here? Are people only in it for the money? Do people really lose creativity because of age?

The second factor is having good questions. These do not need to be complicated to be effective. Below are some good questions to have handy to help in busting premises:

- *How do you/I know that?* (This will uncover any evidence to support the position.)
- *What are you trying to achieve?* (This will elevate the conversation and get back to objectives and not down in the weeds with options.)
- *Why? And why?* (Some quality assurance systems suggest using five "whys" to get to the root cause of the issue. Five may be an overkill, but a couple can help get deeper to the cause.)

The third factor is flexibility. We need to be flexible and ready to adjust with new information. Rigid thinking keeps new information on the outside and values what is known. Flexibility allows people to consider what else they might not know that is pertinent to their situation.

With all three factors, we can be much better at recognizing possible blind spots and getting the true heart of an issue.

Now You're Talkin'

The worst questions are often silent and occur between our own two ears. Destructive self-talk is often phrased in the form of questions. The questions are silent and, unfortunately, they are often on auto-repeat. Martin Seligman, author of *Learned Optimism*, has done a lot to shed a light on this important topic. For a more in-depth look at the subject, I would recommend his book, however at a basic level, self-critical questions often sound like these:

- Am I good enough?
- Who am I (to do/try this)?
- Can people see through me?
- Do I deserve this?
- What if they do not like me (or what I say or what I do)?

These kinds of questions are not just dumb, even worse: they are damaging. They are not really questions, so much as *questioning*. Honest questions are seeking information. Negative self-talk questions are not honest and are not really seeking any answers. Negotiations in bad faith go nowhere. Likewise these questions are being asked in bad faith will take us nowhere good.

Negative self-talk questions also fail horribly if we were to grade them against our chart for raising awareness and forwarding motion. Awareness grows not one iota. Action is usually stymied. Plus, we feel worse about ourselves. Besides that, asking ourselves terrible questions is a wonderful habit.

Getting a strong handle on how we talk to ourselves as essential. Here are some better internal questions:

- If they can do it, why can't I?
- What can I learn from others who are doing what I would love to do?
- Why was I successful at that in the past?
- Why not me?
- Why not our organization/team?

Asking bad questions of ourselves is evidence of an overactive inner critic. What we need are quality questions that support our strengths and enhance motivation. These are the hallmarks of a healthy inner mentor.

The High Art of Impossibility Thinking

We've all come across people (and it may have been us) who were stuck. The situation was negative or undesirable, and yet the person was resistant to the idea that anything can be done by them to change it. The conversation probably went around every point of the compass.

What you may have observed was the high art of impossibility thinking. Impossibility thinking is shutting oneself out from the idea that there is any solution at all. It goes something like this.

Stuck: I don't like this situation.

Trying to help: Why don't you do X?

Stuck: I can't do X because…

Trying to help: Why don't you do Y?

Stuck: I can't do Y because…

…and round it goes.

Untenable situation

More
adaptation
or
justification

Attempts to
adapt or
justify

Feel less
empowered

Deterioration
of condition

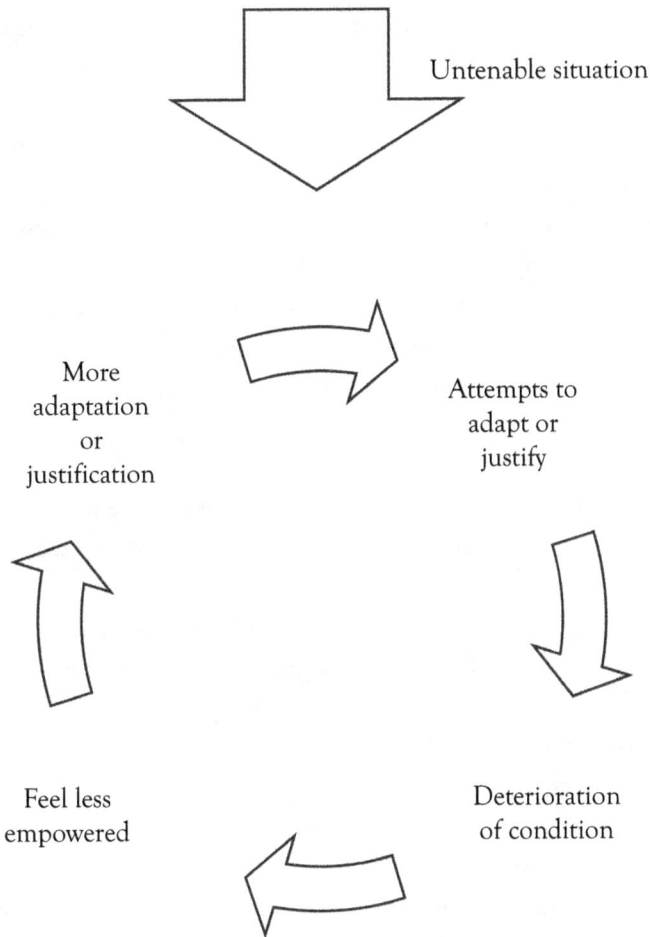

Figure 4.2 Untenable vicious cycles

You can't square a circle. The first problem is that the questions in this scenario were actually just suggestions in the form of a question. Impossibility thinking is like a black hole; it can suck in an infinite number of suggestions and remain unchanged. People say that a boat is a hole in the water into which money is thrown. Likewise, suggestions in the form of questions can forever be poured into an impossibility thinker and have zero effect. The second reason this situation resists resolution is because the person who is "stuck" is not taking responsibility.

Effective questions act like a lever. Levers are extremely powerful. Archimedes understood the power of levers and said, "Give me a long enough lever and a place to put it and I can move the world." Questions act like levers, but they have to be anchored against something. They have to be anchored in solid premises and in solid responsibility.

So, here's a question: How does one cure the impossibility thinking in another? The answer is, you don't. People need to rein in their own justifications. As long as the justifications are plentiful, the options appear limited, and there people will sit.

As can be seen in Figure 4.2 impossibility thinkers get caught in a vicious cycle. As long as they focus their creativity on justifications and inappropriate adaptation strategies, there they will stay.

The vicious cycle includes these basic steps:

1. One attempts to justify or adapt to an unsustainable situation.
2. The condition deteriorates or opportunities to change are lost.
3. The person feels more overwhelmed and less empowered.
4. Adaptations continued and justifications layered or renewed.

Once people are in this loop, they try to explain and externalize the control. The explanations and justifications are plentiful. The case against any option is water-tight, so there is no change. Voila! The person is now riding a vicious cycle.

The cycle needs an interrupt and the interrupt needs to occur at the point of justifying the adaptation. A vicious cycle is perpetuated when people have reasoned that adaptation is the appropriate course. These reasons must be highlighted and removed. Scanners at the airport security pick out objects that require further scrutiny and possible removal. People also need to scan for their justifications and get rid of them.

- Is this really worth it?
- Is this really the best I can do?
- Is this really sustainable?

We can help break that cycle for ourselves and others with better questions that get to the root of issues and burst justifications.

Augmented Intelligence

A change in perspective is a great way to ask better questions. We can try to get that perspective on our own. We can take the team on a retreat. Some companies offer sabbaticals to leaders. We can take a vacation and return to an issue with a fresh set of eyes.

Sometimes it is quicker and more powerful to augment our intelligence with outside help.

The topic of artificial intelligence is ubiquitous. What people tend to miss is that AI should augment and not replace intelligence. There is great benefit to augmenting our own intelligence. Why go it alone? When we are isolated, our options can appear limited.

When we were exploring some caves, I was complaining to my wife about the awful flashlights we had just bought. I said they were junk and just way too dim. I was angry at "being ripped off." She asked me if I felt the dimness had anything to do with the fact that I still had my sunglasses on. Ah, the power of outside perspective!

Untenable situations are at their heart irrational. The operating premise is at best a half truth and often a flat out lie.

- My business will be crushed if she leaves.
- I can't invest now because I have bills.
- There are no jobs here.
- I need another degree or certification before I can get into that field.
- The culture around here does not value good ideas.

An outside perspective can burst the balloon of our assumptions. It can open us up to new alternatives. A good outside perspective will help us to have better answers to questions like these:

- How do you or I know that?
- What am I trying to accomplish here?
- What is a simple way to meet my objective?
- What are some potential obstacles?
- What evidence am I seeing that the current approach is actually working?

An outside perspective will also help to make sure that the answers we give to these questions are not just easy or superficial. An outside perspective will help people to consider new information and dig a bit deeper.

But why do some leaders resist looking for an outside perspective? Here are a few common reasons:

- An overdeveloped sense of independence (the person feels that if their initiative got them this far, then they should continue to rely on it)
- The mistaken belief that asking for help is a sign of weakness (the person feels that since they are the expert they should have all the answers already)
- Falling for the myth that only experts in their field can understand the issue (this ignores the fact that a plethora of experts around the situation has not improved it so far).

Great questions help us see things in a new light and make practical steps forward. Make sure they are working for you, not against you, and are predicated with appropriate responsibility and solid premises.

Summary and Tips

- Dumb questions do exist. Avoid them and diminish their potential impact by evaluating if they are raising awareness and moving things forward.
- Beware false premises. They generate poor questions that can lead to bad answers.
- Avoid the particularly noxious variety of dumb questions that are, in fact, negative self-talk.
- Avoid the effects of impossibility thinking by busting justifications and expanding options.
- Get outside help to augment your native intelligence.

CHAPTER 5

Visualize a Different State

- You can't out-train a poor diet and you can't outperform a lousy vision.
- The three disciplines of vision
- Vision: direction and fuel for the road
- The bigger context

Many talk about the importance of vision as a destination. What is often missed is the fact that vision is the upper control limit to performance: can't see it, can't do it. The more vivid a state is made, the more energy and excitement there will be to get moving. A great vision acts as both the compass and the energy to get moving.

You Can't Out-Train a Poor Diet and You Can't Outperform a Lousy Vision

Most of my life, I have been on the thin side. People would often say I looked like a runner even when I was not running much. Wanting to bulk up, I decided to avoid cardio, started lifting hard, and gave myself permission to eat anything I wanted. My 40-year-old body ballooned immediately—and right in the middle. My daughter asked, "Dad, why did you get so fat?"

The answer was that while I trained hard, there was just no way to offset the effects of an awful diet. Likewise, there is no way to perform at a high level with a low vision. Vision is the upper control limit of performance.

There are some limited exceptions. A mother will defend a child from a wild animal she might otherwise run from. There are piano prodigies who just start playing Mozart as toddlers. More commonly, vision plays a huge role in determining how well we will eventually perform and even what we will attempt.

If someone sees themselves as someone who is bad at math, it is very hard for them to improve. A person who does not see themselves as someone who can speak in public will have a tough time doing well in front of an audience. A person who does not see themselves as a leader may struggle to improve (and may never put themselves in a position where they may be called to lead in the first place). A person who does not see themselves as athletic may never try to take up athletic pursuits. A person who does not see themselves as creative may not try to drive innovation or tap into their creativity. A person who does not see themselves as someone with something to say will struggle to speak up.

Bradley Cooper was nominated for a Golden Globe for directing the movie *A Star Is Born*. If his vision was limited to being an actor, he may not have tried his hand at something new. Tyler Perry produced the "Madea" comedy movie franchise and created hundreds of millions of dollars in ticket sales through his own production company. If his vision was limited to acting, he may not have attempted to build a studio empire.

Just as an individual's performance is limited by vision, so too are organizations. What would Apple look like if they had thought of themselves as just a desktop or laptop manufacturer? What would a national restaurant chain look like if they thought they could only make it in their own state? Where would Southwest Airlines be if their vision was limited to playing second fiddle to the traditional carriers? Vision in these cases not only enabled a destination but enhanced performance along the way. Any growth to a new level requires grit, innovation, resilience, and smarts, which can only be brought into play with appropriate vision.

A poor organizational vision can degrade performance. Unproductive beliefs will start to creep in and affect the ability to execute at a higher level. These might include beliefs like: "we are not creative enough," or "we can't really compete at that level," or "we are excellent at X and cannot get any better at Y."

At this point, it is important to highlight the dynamic between vision and experience. Vision is necessary for high performance, but vision alone is insufficient. People also need to cultivate the experience and skills to get where they need to go. Think of vision as the upper control limit of performance and skills/experience as the lower control limit. See the diagram below.

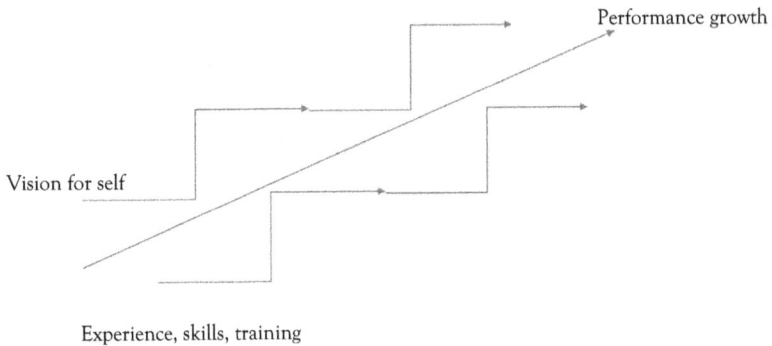

Figure 5.1 **Performance growth cycle**

Figure 5.1 illustrates the relationship between upper control limit and lower control limit. A person cannot escape the reality of their current, real ability. In the military, there is a saying that people under pressure do not rise to the occasion, they sink to their level of training. A person can have a great vision to compete well in a marathon, but with insufficient training, they will fall short, cramp up, or otherwise hit the wall and "bonk."

The phenomenon of sinking to one's level of training is hard to miss in a fight. Just look at any mixed martial arts match-up. When a fighter is getting pressured, they revert to the combinations or techniques they know best. A great wrestler getting lit up by punches and kicks from their opponent will try and take the fight to the ground. Someone with a strong right punch might lean on that to get a one punch knockout instead of using combinations.

The pattern is apparent in professional settings too. A leader who always got success in the past by "being hands on" may fall back on a directive style when things do not immediately go his way. A leader might go back to reading PowerPoint presentations after a disappointing attempt to use storytelling in corporate presentations. Organizations perennially bounce between distributing decision-making authority to business units or regions and then change course and pull that authority back to the head office when too much cohesion was lost.

People will often give up on visioning because they neglect the experience side of the equation. Like a "yo-yo dieter," they get skeptical of any kind of food regimen after repeated failures. We can see examples of this every year when people make their New Year's resolutions. A month or two go great and then they fall off the wagon. People who have had issues with their visions not being realized might become disenchanted with the idea of visioning. The problem is not visioning, which is eminently practical, but it is people ignoring the fact they need to work on getting the experience, knowledge, and training to bridge that gap.

The Three Disciplines of Vision

Effective visions require vision discipline. The three elements of vision discipline are vision setting, vision visibility, and vision vitality.

The first discipline is setting visions actively. Having a vision is not the same as setting a vision. I had a meal at a national restaurant chain that happened to be a client and had a nice chat with the cashier. She told me about her plans to go to school to be a dental assistant. "Are you interested in dentistry?" I asked. She explained her mother thought it would be a good idea. The young lady now had a vision, but not the one she had developed. The best visions are ones we actively set ourselves, not just put on like a borrowed hat.

In my opinion, I think the vision was too small a vision for her. I had seen just how outgoing she was with customers. Plus she was standing in the middle of the retail part of the restaurant and saying, "I just love to sell." But whether the vision came from her mother of the vision came from me, neither would be optimal for her. Her best results would come with her active involvement in her own destiny. We have to have skin in the game. Especially if it is our own skin and our own game.

It is best to set our own visions. Even if that vision is not ideal, it is still better than visions provided by others. Consider the impact of the well-meaning parent who maps out a child's career plan with limited or zero input from the child. How many people have you seen dispiritedly following the path laid out by others? Or perhaps you have seen those that run in rebellion at the first opportunity? Beware imposed visions.

This same caution also applies when setting goals for people. In a work context, the best goals are codesigned between the manager and the employee. Rarely will imposed goals (e.g., "your goal is to be more assertive") work out.

Also note the step shape of the graph. It reflects the natural progression of how people develop. There are periods where a vision for ourselves suddenly spikes up even though our experience is not there yet. This can be seen vividly in the years around high school and after as people get into the professional world or college. There was likely a point at which a parent, mentor, or counselor said something like "I can see you being an engineer." As soon as we hear and agree with a statement like that, our vision for ourselves has gone up a step. Our skills and experience are lagging, but education and work experience will be there to reconcile the gap. This is how people naturally progress: they get an idea they can do better, then they get the experience to bridge the gap. Where this gets really interesting is using this process on purpose. Purposefully raising our vision and purposefully taking steps to close the gap. Too often we can get lazy and stop using the natural techniques that elevated our growth so effectively as younger people.

We can gain enormous leverage by getting back into the habit of raising visions and closing gaps. A leader should intentionally and regularly raise their vision for themselves in specific areas of performance like speaking or being more influential. A team should intentionally and regularly raise their vision for themselves in specific areas like collaboration or innovation.

The second part of vision discipline is to keep it *visible*. One cannot just "set it and forget it" when it comes to vision. It needs to be attended to and remembered. You might find that you are off track. You might find you have exceeded expectations. You might find the vision no longer suits.

Too often people make a vision and then hang it up like a suit in the back of the closet. The only beneficiaries of that strategy will be the moths. In the case of visions, out of sight is out of mind. And out of mind will put us out of the contest. Visions need to be made what I call semipermanent. They at least need to be written down and recorded but not carved in stone.

The third discipline is vision *vitality*. Vision can deteriorate over time. Like any fine-tuned tool, a vision needs routine maintenance. Lack of use is bad for visions. Even vintage cars that are fervently protected from the weather need to have the engine started once in a while. Thoroughbred horses need to get to the track to stay in prime condition. As the saying goes, a boat is safe at harbor, but that is not what boats are made for. Likewise, we need to exercise our visions for them to be the useful tool we need them to be.

Vision vitality is maintained by regularly:

Evaluating for changes in events or conditions. What has changed that might have an impact?

Evaluating assumptions. Are there any assumptions that were inaccurate, overblown, or underappreciated?

Reviewing progress and successes. What has been achieved and what factors contributed to that successes? Can these be exploited further?

Incorporating and learning from setbacks. What was not achieved? What was the root cause and what can be learned?

Integrating high-quality feedback. What are respected mentors and experts telling us about pace, quality, and quantity of results?

Keeping in touch with what you really want. Is the direction still relevant and meaningful to you?

Visions can be incredibly beneficial, but they do need some discipline to make them work most effectively.

Vision: Direction and Fuel for the Journey

Great visions not only act as a compass, they also act as the fuel. I often talk to people about alacrity. Alacrity is moving with both speed and enthusiasm. Enthusiasm comes from feelings of fulfillment and pride of progress. These are natural by-products of taking action on a worthy vision.

A chronic lack of enthusiasm should be a red flag. Of course, any of us will get tired or discouraged from time to time, but our vision should be producing some level of excitement in us. If is not, then we need to rethink where we are going. We want to move fast, but speed without joy will only result in a hollow accomplishment and a lonely journey.

The process of setting a vision gives us fuel for the times when it feels like no obvious progress is being made. It fuels us when the inevitable setbacks occur.

Energy from vision is personally tailored. Ideal nutrition is slightly different for each body; we all metabolize, digest, and utilize nutritional components somewhat differently. Some things that are excellent sources of nutrition for you can cause an allergic reaction in someone else. Likewise, the fuel from a particular vision is only ideal to those that created it.

I am fascinated by obituaries, not because I am curious about how people died, but because I am curious about how people lived. *The Wall Street Journal* does a particularly good job each week of highlighting three notable people that have passed away. There are a wide range of things that can make a person notable. Some were notable businesspeople. Some were notable artists or authors. Some were notable for their civic involvements. While there are some that were notable due to accident or some historic coincidence, most are notable because of their achievements and contributions. These people each had a unique perspective on how they would like to live their life. What motivated them may not motivate me or you.

A vision created by you for you (or by your team and for your team) should create feelings of excitement and enthusiasm. If it does not, it is time for a rethink.

The Bigger Context

Taking time to set or reset visions is an incredibility important part of handling untenable situations. A vision will show an untenable situation in stark relief. The untenable situation will either look like an anchor to where we want to go or a key obstacle with which we must deal. When the tide recedes, it is clear who was naked. When we get a clear vision, we can tell where we are at odds from where we want to be and then we can take the actions that will get us back on course.

Visioning is a strategic activity and will keep us out of the weeds and focused on the important, not just the urgent. Strategy formulation in its simplest form is determining the future state, describing the current state, and identifying the critical issues that will aid or prevent getting to the future state. Done correctly, visioning can help identify gaps for leaders and their organizations to take key actions quickly and decisively.

Let's take a look at the steps and some examples.

Step 1: Get clear on B. B is our destination.

Step 2: Get real on A. A is our current state relative to B.

Step 3: Get specific on critical issues. Critical issues are those things that must be addressed (not necessarily the answers) to bridge the gap.

A person who was interested in boosting their fitness might look at it like this:

Get clear on B: I want to be able to finish a marathon in under five hours with combination of running and walking.

Get real on A: Can currently run about two to three miles and feel good. Have completed a half-marathon in three hours.

Get clear on critical issues: I have trouble following a training regimen and have finished shorter race distances in the past, but mostly result of "winging it."

This person might consider a run club or trainer to help with account-ability and ensure that the longer training is done and done correctly.

Let's look at the example of a leader who wants to be more productive at work and not merely busy.

Get clear on B: The leader would be proactively working on important, but not necessarily urgent issues and handling tactical day-to-day issues in an efficient manner.

Get real on A: The leader is currently experiencing a hectic day-to-day schedule characterized by a reactive mode.

Get specific on critical issues: These might include working on 10 priorities, key top talent has left or is at risk of leaving, and lack of effective collabo-ration between business units.

This leader would want to look at ways to address the number or order of the priorities, have a strategy to address the talent risks, and look at options to ensure collaboration.

The process of setting and reviewing vision on a regular basis high-lights when we are off course from where we want to go, not making the progress we want, or if conditions have changed that will affect the trajectory. This process is valuable to individual leaders, their teams, and their organizations. There is value in both seeing any deviations and also validating that the current course and actions are appropriate.

Summary and Tips

- When setting vision, also address the current state of reality to highlight gaps.
- Be sure the vision you set belongs to you.
- Keep your vision visible and part of daily activities.
- Update your vision regularly by including feedback from the environment and trusted others.
- Evaluate the vision for the degree of enthusiasm it is generating.
- Use vision to help expose the existence and significance of possible untenable situations.

CHAPTER 6

Not All Hurdles Are on the Outside

- Extreme self-trust and do you look funny on your horse?
- The back-seat barrier
- Past as a precursor
- The blame game
- Whale talk and the Jonah complex

Not all barriers to a situation will be due to external factors. There is a rich world of inner barriers that contribute to untenable situations. These inner barriers and the beliefs that sustain them must be addressed to make progress. This chapter describes the surprising inner conditions that are related to untenable situations.

Extreme Self-Trust and Do You Look Funny on Your Horse?

You can't lead a Calvary charge if you think you look funny on a horse.
—John Peers

Not only does high performance require vision for the future, it also requires belief. Lack of belief can cause people to slow down, quit, or never even try. Lack of self-trust can cause or perpetuate untenable situations.

An overconcern with looking funny can also shut down our creativity. It can keep us hugging the trunk of the tree instead of venturing out on a limb. Some of the most enjoyable aspects of life are the result of someone not being constrained by the fear of looking funny.

I am glad that John Denver was not shy about his thankfulness for being a country boy. Aren't we glad that Jim Henson was not too serious to play with puppets? Think of the millions of people who would not have enjoyed the escape to the magical world of Harry Potter if J. K. Rowling had dismissed her stories as just "silly" and hid them away.

Aside from the few examples of awful singers trying out for big-time TV talent shows, most people do not suffer from too much trust in themselves. In fact, it is quite the opposite: the vast majority of people underestimate themselves. The majority of people are not jumping up and saying they should be president, or governor, or mayor. The majority of people are not even pushing themselves forward to be leaders in their own circle.

Just as most people could be two times more assertive and still come across as nice people, most people could still be two times more trusting of themselves and still be well within the realm of reality. They need to get more extreme about their self-trust.

In the case of people with little talent trying out for the TV talent shows, the world will clearly tell them they are not very good. Judges will tell them. They will not get invited to sing on stage for money. People will not want to listen to them even for free. If they can improve their craft with singing coaches or get more experience, that would be great, but if not, reasonable people will see their level of talent and make some decisions.

For most of us, though, we're just in the area of normal work and life. Our talents (or lack of talents) are not so immediately drastic or apparent. What is apparent are the opportunities that are lost for people just because they are afraid of looking silly. A person who is only slightly reticent about their worth can forgo hundreds of thousands of dollars in income in their career. They can pigeonhole themselves in safe if not very interesting or dynamic roles.

Cars come with speedometers that end with an upper limit. By contrast, a person's upper limit is not printed anywhere. Yet some people put a ridiculously low limit on their speedometer with no proof whatsoever.

Rental moving trucks have "governors" on the engine that limits how fast they can go. People too can put artificial governors that put a brake on their own progress. They let beliefs that they might "look silly" dampen their momentum.

People know that they should probably trust themselves more, but even if they do, they are way below where they out to be. Seriously, most people could trust themselves 2x more and still be within the realm of possibility and far away from any delusions of grandeur.

The Back-Seat Barrier

There is a specific kind of limiting belief that I call the back-seat barrier. It occurs when people are confronted with situations where it is possible that others could step in. The limiting belief is that other more qualified, certain, capable people should handle it, and not them. They put themselves in the back seat.

People can believe this despite the fact that there is no correlation between certainty and being correct. People can be very certain and yet still be very wrong. People can appear to be very qualified and yet be complete disasters. Read the business papers for any length of time and you will see that some take the reins with big fanfare only to be ushered out quietly by the board in a couple of years. A prime example was the CEO hired to fix JCPenney, who (with high certainty and little input) got rid of coupons and sales. It turned out that die-hard JCPenney shoppers loved these coupons and when the results disappointed, he was out shortly thereafter.

People with high confidence are not bothered by this belief. Neither are people with overconfidence. The real loss occurs when people who should and could make a difference hesitate or defer to others. Not everyone is qualified. True, but too many hang back and wait for others. Maybe the person to resolve the situation should be you.

To be clear, when I am talking about "should" here, I am not talking about guilt. Rather, it is important for people to take a healthy look at the situation and determine if they might be the appropriate or perhaps ideal person to help resolve it.

Here are some criteria to consider whether this is a "you should take the wheel" situation:

- You played a key role in the root cause.
- You can clearly see the root cause.
- You are the appropriate remedy or can provide the appropriate remedy.
- Your involvement fits your role of responsibility (parent, manager, neighbor, etc.).
- Your involvement would help you grow or overcome a fear or inhibition.

- You would benefit by a quick resolution and high-quality resolution of the situation.

Too many people let their estimation of themselves put them in a back-seat position. This is especially damaging in organizations when leaders that need to be taking a more proactive role sabotage themselves and take a less active stance than what the situation requires. People need to be more extreme in their self-trust and one specific way they can manifest that is to get in the driver's seat and take more appropriate control.

Past as a Precursor

The past can either be fuel or a barrier to resolving issues. Let's examine the past as a fuel first.

My grandfather, like many other grandfathers, had a habit of telling stories about his successes. He would tell stories about how after the war they had to make their parts for trucks to operate in Japan because no supplies were readily available. He would tell stories about the power of showing up and luck. According to him, he became the top salesperson at John Hancock in part because of a fortuitous tap on the shoulder from an oil man at his Kiwanis club who needed insurance.

Consider some of the people that you consider successes. Even the humblest of them are likely have some good things to say about themselves. Most successful people have a rich library of success stories. If you were around them long enough (like with family members) you will start to see them repeat. Sometimes hearing the success stories of others can get stale over time. However, the success stories we tell ourselves never get stale. They never lose their nutritional value. These success nuggets are incredibly healthy fuel and a great asset to resolve issues.

Stories are good for others to learn. But stories have incredible power for the owner. They help us remember strengths and give us the fuel to move forward. Yet too many people have some pretty dumb stories they keep telling themselves. They can take the wrong lessons from their history.

People will often observe others and think if they can do it I certainly can. That is pretty positive thinking and a useful mind-set. What's even more powerful is using our own stories as the *justification* for being able to do even bigger things or to take on newer challenges. That is using a personal history as a positive precursor.

Movie trailers do an excellent job of marketing movies. Trailers are a snapshot of all the best parts of the movie and are designed to put the movie in the best light and get people in the seats. People get a preview of what the movie is about and decide if it is going to be good or not. No marketer ever intended to put a bad trailer together. They always try to put together a compelling arrangement.

Are you making good trailers or bad trailers? Good trailers will talk about the connection between past successes and how these may play a part in the future. Bad trailers will aggregate past failures and use them to explain the likelihood of failure or become some kind of documentary evidence as to why we should not attempt something new or attempt something again.

People can take their "bad" past and make that the precursor of their future. They can put up their own historical barriers.

Make sure your past is supportive of your future and not an impediment. Everyone has made mistakes. Everyone has instances where they have not performed at their highest level. It takes a small person to let those past mistakes and failures cast a shadow on the future. It takes a bigger person to admit to an imperfection and not let it morph into an excuse. Diamonds with flaws are still diamonds and useful for both their aesthetics and for their cutting power.

Exercise

Make your own success trailers. What are some examples of you stepping up and being your best? List three or more instances in which you played a pivotal role of an improved condition for you or others.

The Blame Game

This internal roadblock often masquerades as one or more external roadblocks. People can blame external factors like the weather, the economy, the upbringing, or the boss. Yes, many of these factors are critical issues, but they are not the issue themselves.

Blame is an easy out and an awful habit. The act of blaming others or conditions leaves the blamer as the one paralyzed. It's like a snake suffering from the effects of its own poison.

When I coach people, their relationship with and the behavior of their boss is often a key factor. The people I coach have things they want to do or accomplish, but the wants and needs of the boss must be taken into account as well. The leader–supervisor relationship is a critical issue to address, but the behavior of their leader cannot be the excuse. We have to work within and do the best we can with the situation we have. It is an easy excuse to say my boss, my organization, or my leadership is too stupid to see my great ideas and then just take my ball and go home. We need to look and see what else we can do to improve or best deal with the conditions.

A bad economy with companies hiring a fewer people may be a fact, but it cannot be an excuse. In 2008, at the height of the recession, my wife's friend decided she needed to make a career move. While others were saying "there are no jobs," she was getting interviews all over. She just went out to find what opportunities there were and make things happen instead of sitting around and waiting for the economy to improve.

High performers see that they have a high degree of control over their actions even when the environment is not conducive.

Despite every possible excuse, Mansour Bahrami became a popular tennis player. He grew up in Iran under modest circumstances, where under the Shah, only the elites and the rich could play. After the Shah was deposed, tennis was seen as a polluting Western influence and nobody could play. Bahrami spent most of his young life playing "tennis" with improvised equipment like pots and pans. He became a skilled player, but also developed a large repertoire of trick shots. So he went to France with no money and through grit, talent, and a bit of luck, he was able to create a career in tennis for himself. If he had just stayed home and waited for a help wanted ad in the paper for "tennis trick shot expert and semi-pro entertainer," he would still be waiting.

The surprising part about this is that people know they should not blame others or the external conditions, but it is tempting and often addictive to do so. People can let blame take outsize control and diminish their own power.

It is a short trip from blaming to self-pity. Success cannot grow in soil polluted with self-pity. Animals in my observation don't seem to get drugged down by self-pity. A cow in a freezing field may not look happy, but doesn't seem to waste time railing at the poor fate of cows. They just get on with whatever cows do.

Water coolers and coffee break areas are hot zones for blame and self-pity. If they had ears, I would feel sorry for the coffee machines, water dispensers, and refrigerators that are subjected to ongoing streams of commiseration about how dumb the organization is and how managers do not listen to smart ideas. It is true many organizations seem tone deaf to good ideas. But it is also sheer laziness to expect that the brilliance of an idea will be immediately evident. People will make lazy attempts at influence then turn around and blame the dumb organization or their leader for not being open to good ideas. It is silly and disempowering.

While some will blame, the world is full of examples of success and accomplishment without the excuses. In Colorado, there are pieces of mining equipment in the most improbable and inhospitable places. When I was on a mine tour, it was pointed out that at the tip of the mountain we were about to go inside, there was a tiny rectangle. Astoundingly, that rectangle, thousands of feet up on the ridge of a mountain, was in fact an enormous bunkhouse to house miners. The amount of grit and ingenuity to build a structure in a place like that is startling to consider. Every excuse could have been found (the altitude, the cold, the lightning, the wind) and yet somebody decided to just get it done and did it.

Our daily existence may not be fraught with perils like that of miners, but people can still give up too much power. The main issue is to what extent will we allow untenable conditions to exist by blaming others or are conditions for not taking appropriate steps to address. The opposite of blaming is responsibility.

Playing the blame game may take the pressure off the individual for the moment, but it is a temporary respite. The untenable situation still exists and deteriorates.

Whale Talk and the Jonah Complex

Abraham Maslow is famous for his thoughts on the "hierarchy of needs," but he also wrote about what he called the Jonah complex. The Jonah complex occurs when a person does not take steps out of fear that they may not live up to a standard. The phrase comes from the biblical story of Jonah, who was called upon by God, but tried to hide away. He ended up in the belly of a big fish. Just like people can fear failure, people can also fear success. And try to run from it.

On a ladder, people can feel secure on the initial steps, but start to feel trepidation on subsequent steps. No matter how secure the ladder feels, the sense of height and the sense of exposure starts to come in and they hold back.

Climbing on ladders can have real physical consequences, but for most people, the conditions they are avoiding hold no physical danger. They hesitate to climb even when there is no real downside.

People can feel they are not special enough. They can feel they don't have "it," whatever "it" is. The feeling can keep people on the lower rungs. The feeling can keep people from trying. Whale talk can psych us out if we let it. Let's not let it.

When I was a kid, family friends had horses and ponies. One of my earliest memories is riding double on the back of a little white pony named Sugar. I would ride double with the daughter of the family friends (she called the pony "Booger"), who was the same age as me. She had the reins, but I was nervous and intentionally slipped off the back and down Booger's rump to get off.

Nothing bad was happening. The pony wasn't bucking. The terrain was unchanged. Booger was as steady as a four-post bed with hooves. I tried to pass it off as an accident, but my friend didn't buy it. I wasn't scared in that moment; I was just scared of what might happen if I stayed on too long. That's a Jonah complex.

Thankfully I was shamed into getting back on Booger, but how many times do we slide off opportunity and avoid the opportunity at hand?

There are obvious disadvantages and some insidious "advantages" to sliding off an opportunity.

The disadvantages are obvious:

- You will not achieve the potential (e.g., you will never be a cowboy).
- You will miss out on the benefits of accomplishment (e.g., you will never ride with a cowgirl).

But there are some insidious advantages:

- Your ego will remain undamaged (e.g., you can always console yourself that you are a good walker).
- You will not stand out (and no one will ask more of you).
- You cannot be accused of thinking more of yourself than others do.

This dynamic is why it is so important for us to listen to the encouragement of others and just soak it in like sunshine on a leaf, but analyze feedback with some discernment. There is hardly any downside to working on self-perceived potential. Feedback on our limits is worthy of consideration, but should be taken with a grain of salt. If the Jonah complex is at work with us, it can also be at work in others and that can impact the kind of feedback we get from others.

It is common to hear the statement that people fear public speaking more than they fear death. If we believe that, then people can feel safe behind the "norm" if they do not try. Whale talk is that inner dialogue that keeps us in place and (as Figure 6.1 shows) working well below our potential.

Here is what whale talk can sound like:

- I'm not the kind of person to put myself forward.
- Other people are more capable.
- Who am I to aspire to that?
- What if I can't do the next thing?
- What if I try, but I disappoint people?
- What will my friends/family think?
- That next level just doesn't seem like it is for me.
- Who are you to be great at anything?
- But I will have to give up what I am comfortable with today.

Glass ceilings can exist in organizations, but the first ceiling to address is one's belief in one's own ability. A colleague works in finance at a global manufacturing company. From her position, she saw opportunities that would create enormous benefit in management of the supply chain. Unfortunately, she did not speak up because she assumed others must know more about the subject than she did. She thought she must

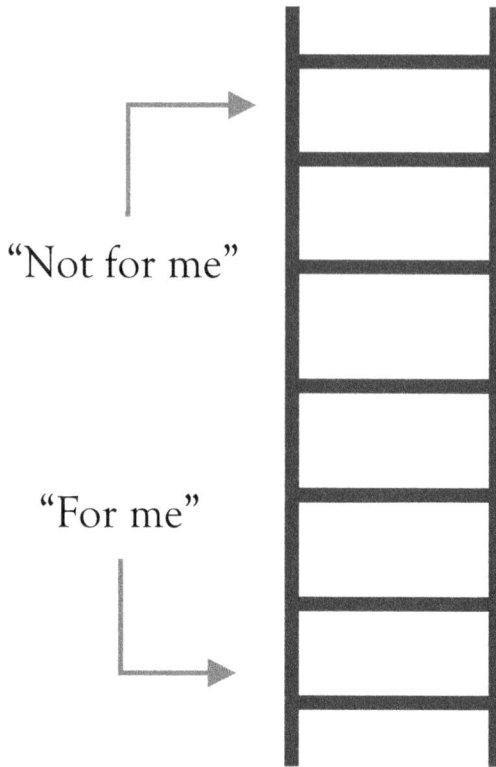

Figure 6.1 Whale talk

be missing something. After taking executive education classes in supply chain management, she realized she already knew quite a bit that would have been valuable. Yet she had hesitated and waited for the validation of a class to prop her confidence up. The whale talk got to her.

Maslow said that people "must have the arrogance of creativity." Breaking out of the whale talk does require a little arrogance. For the vast majority of people, they are at little risk of jumping to the extremes of hubris and self-delusion. Most people are naturally steered away from that extreme by the gravity of humility. Effectively managing the whale talk allows people to explore the upper limit without being pulled down unnecessarily by the omnipresent gravity of their own self-doubt, internalized comforts, and humility.

In Chapter 5, I introduced the concept of upper control limits and lower control limits and their effect on performance. Whale talk will push down the upper control limit of how we see ourselves. Whale talk can twist reality, and give us reasonable sounding excuses to avoid the exercising of our talents. In the world of work, the likeliest casualty of not living up to a standard will be a bruised ego, which can be remarkably resilient if we let them.

In the movie *The Princess Bride*, one of the villains (who has abducted the Princess Buttercup) repeatedly uses the phrase "inconceivable!" every time the hero outmaneuvers him. He could not conceive that others might be smarter than him. He cannot believe things are happening when they are. Whale talk and the Jonah complex is all about incomprehension. We cannot believe we have the talents or that we are somehow inferior to others even before we start. It may turn out we are in fact inferior to others in different ways, but a person will never know if they do not try. Almost any interview with a successful person will elicit the reflection "I never imagined I would get this far." Yet, along their journey they still took another step on the rung and tested their abilities. If they had let their thinking prevent them from taking that next step, it would have been a self-fulfilling prophecy.

Summary and Tips

Internal barriers do exist. Be rigorous in your assessment of the barriers and take proactive steps to address.

Assess for yourself for any internal barriers:

- Do you hold yourself back out of fear of looking silly?
- Have you over-externalized control of the situation?
- Are you allowing past failures to unnecessarily impact current activity?
- Do you or your team waste time with self-pity or commiseration?
- Do you allow whale talk to put an upper limit on your vision for yourself?

CHAPTER 7

Taking Steps. Break Mountains into Mole-Hills

- Objects may not be as close as they appear.
- Getting granular
- How to do 100 burpees
- Preparing "as if" (running shoes on the floor and alarm set)

Progress against untenable situations is about taking a "right-sized" approach. Too often these situations are blown out of proportion. The task seems too big. The immensity immobilizes. When we right-size we can take those next steps and gain traction.

Objects May Not Be as Close as They Appear

We have all seen the warning on automobile side-view mirrors: objects may be closer than they appear. It's a good reminder of the distortive effects of a mirror. Our minds can also have a distortive effect. Our minds can make both situations and consequences look much bigger than they really are.

Many will have experienced a time when the idea of getting a job or working at a big corporation may have seemed daunting. Then we get into it and likely find that is was much more manageable than we thought. It is like The Wizard of Oz pulling back the curtains.

Writing that first book may look too big. Being in that first play may seem too big. Calling that first girl for a date may look like a big deal. (Actually I do not think that fear ever totally vanishes.) Being able to present to the board of directors may seem like a big deal. Starting that first marathon at the beginning of 26.2 miles can look like an impossible task.

Fear makes things bigger in our field of vision. That is a good thing when a truck is barreling down at us. We need to see that truck. But fear can make loads of other things look bigger than they have a right to be— even when we're at no real risk.

An Ironman distance triathlon is a 2.4-mile swim, 112-mile bike, and 26.2-mile run. One of my friends did six in 14 months. He kept trying to get me to commit to doing one. I demurred. He conceded that the training is hard, but insisted it really was more of a mental game than a physical one. He said you just swim, bike, or run to the next thing. He is right. Joggers will often use a trick of running to the next lamp post or the next water station in a race. On a long business trip, road warriors will focus on the next flight leg to get them home or to the next appointment.

To make progress on big things, it is important to get perspective. Everyone knows not to make mountains out of molehills but sometimes we make hills out of even less or nothing at all. It is important to realize that buying into the bigness of a problem does not have anything to do with us being able to solve it.

It is essential to get things into manageable chunks. We can do this quickly and reduce the size of a problem by focusing on the *obvious next step*.

For what the obvious next step might be, we need to figure out the cause of the problem. Maybe we need to make a decision. Maybe we need to make a plan. The choices are actually not as vast as we might think.

A person cannot boil an ocean, but they can take the parts of the ocean they need. Sailboats have an ingenious device called a water maker. Even a small ship in the middle of the mighty Pacific can produce water with the right equipment and some electricity. You cannot boil the ocean and likely do not need to with the right approach. My observation is that many people will not only look at situations and magnify the issue's size, they will also magnify the issue's complexity. I see leaders get stuck because they feel they must fix everything when there are likely just one or two things they should focus on to improve the situation.

Do all people in the organization really need training or is it limited to a specific geography? Does the organization really need all new processes or just tightening up a specific process? Do we really need more software to ensure compliance or do we just need specific managers doing a better job ensuring compliance in their departments? Some things need big thinking to fix, but sometimes we just need to isolate and attack specific issues to make progress. Antibodies in a human immune system work so well because they are targeted. They find those things that don't belong and get rid of them selectively. We too can make quick progress on big things by getting specific and taking action where needed.

Breaking things down into digestible chunks is the first and most rational step. At the dinner table, we all realize we need to get things down to bite-size pieces. Why then do we forget this when faced with a big thing?

The key steps to getting granular are similar to the visioning steps outlined in Chapter 5. Here we simply add a fourth step—creating some obvious next steps.

1. *Clarify the objective.* This should be a clear articulation of the future state. For example, you may want high-powered effective senior team or more ideas that actually get implemented. (Hint: use positive objectification. Positive objectification is focusing on what outcome you want, not what you were trying to avoid. Positive: attract or retain the best and brightest talent. Negative: keep from losing people.)

2. *Identify your current state.* Simply answer the question: *Relative to your desired future state, how would you describe where you are currently?*

3. *Identify the critical issues.* In the gap between where you are today and your desired future state, what are the critical issues that must be addressed?

4. *Create some obvious next steps.* An obvious next step (ONS) is simply the quickest and most effective way to move forward and make the condition incrementally better. For example, if one of the critical issues is "unclear as to what really motivates my top talent," then the ONS is to create a plan to find out.

If a person follows this simple process, they will be able to break the issue down to manageable chunks, get an effective plan, and get moving. The key is not to overcomplicate. Keep the activities focused on the critical issues to address. Don't think of all the things you *could* do, but consider the critical few things you *must* do.

My parents take pride in setting a beautiful dinner table. They've got dishes they have collected. They have all the right settings. Napkins are folded or have a ring around them. There is usually a nice centerpiece. I like that they take the time to make things nice, but sometimes you just need to grab a sandwich and get the calories in the body. You don't need to overcomplicate.

How To Do 100 Burpees

There is a power in making incremental progress on things. Anyone who has huffed up a mountain knows the surprise of turning around and seeing how far they have come.

Due to the cross-functional exercise trend over the last several years, many people have become familiar with an exercise called the burpee. It is a basic calisthenic exercise that involves dropping to the ground and jumping back up. Most people hate burpees, but they are a great conditioning exercise. Some people can blast right through a set of burpees, but for many, burpees are a challenge. A hundred burpees is not a lot of fun and a good metaphor for a hard task. How does one approach a hard task like 100 burpees (or 1,000 burpees, if you are a beast)?

Here are a couple of thoughts:

- *Don't psych yourself out from the outset.* Don't let it get too big. Even a marathon is only four to six hours of effort for many recreational athletes.
- *Don't think you have to get through it all at once.* It is impossible to get big things done immediately anyway. The attitude should be to just do one more repetition.
- *Don't hold your breath.* Tough things take energy over time. Maintain that energy through pacing and keeping a pace that you can breathe through.
- *Don't fear sweating.* Hard work and being uncomfortable is part of the territory of growth.

- *Don't think, it won't hurt.* Actually, it's good to imagine what your response will be when it does hurt or starts to get uncomfortable.
- *Smile and add some humor in the moment.* Keep it light and enjoy your efforts.
- *Celebrate each rep.* A little chatter and self-talk helps. It's good to tell yourself "got another" or "just got ten."
- *Don't do alone if you can avoid it.* There is a power that comes from joint activity. If your goal is something can be done in the context of support supportive others, include them.

These same tips can be applied to your big thing, whether the objective is improved health, leadership development, or organizational change.

My first Olympic distance triathlon was full of surprises. My buddy basically dared me to do it, so with very little training or preparation, we registered and showed up. An Olympic distance is nothing compared to an Ironman distance, but it does start with a 1,000-meter swim. This was to be done in a lake. I had not even swum 100 meters in a pool in years, let alone 1,000 meters out in an open body of water.

Race day started in the dark and it was cold. An official told everyone it was time and to swim to the start line in the middle of the lake for a static start. We jumped into the freezing water and I nearly hyperventilated, but made it to the start line and bobbed in the darkness. Once there, a voice from shore said we will start in *"five more minutes."* Incredulous, we just treaded water in the middle of that dark, cold lake. Finally, the start was signaled and off we went toward a large triangle-shaped buoy in the half light of dawn.

How did I not drown? Having a buddy helped. That keeps spirits up. Having no choice helped. The path was out and back. Simply sticking to it helped. Having a cadence helped. Just left arm, right arm and then left arm, right arm.

People generally avoid being in uncomfortable situations, but we've all been there and we all know the drill. We can do things when forced. And when forced, we can keep things simple. And when we keep things simple, we can stay focused until we reach the goal.

Think about how productive most people are before leaving work for vacation. Most get more done in the last two days before vacation than in any other two days in a month. Why is that? I think it is because they focused on the essential. They focused on what they had to do and did not fritter the time away on lower priority items. Would that we applied that focus and simplicity more often. Why not make things "pre-vacation simple" all the time?

There are a few possible reasons for why people make things too complicated:

- Planning something complicated can provide cover for procrastination.
- Lack of trust in one's own common sense and observations.
- Ingrained with the idea that things need to be perfect prior to starting.
- Obscures possibly harsh realities like the person/organization simply not having the discipline to execute.
- The desire to solve all things with a grand plan versus a good plan.

Keeping things simple should be our default position. It allows us to conserve energy for the essential. We know to keep things simple under pressure. We should resist the temptation to make things complex just because we feel like we have the option to do so.

Exercise: The Obvious Next Step(s)

Think about a situation you would like to see improved. Use the three steps outlined above (getting clear on objectives, getting real on current state, and highlighting critical issues). Based on the critical issues, what are the obvious next steps? For example, if there is a problem to fix, do you know the root cause? If not, then the obvious next step is to find the cause. Find the most simple next step that addresses the critical issues raised.

Summary and Tips

- Beware of the distortive effects that can make a task or objective appear too big.
- Break things down into obvious next steps.
- Apply principles of what gets people through tough physical challenges.
- Make simple your default position.

CHAPTER 8

Discover and Rediscover Your Inner Fighter

- Daily assertiveness
- Defining standards
- Taking a stand
- Overplaying helpful

The untenable situation may need us to dig in and take a stand—fight for what is valued. Too many people are passive and ignore setting standards for themselves. They let the standards of others take over and influence their moves.

Daily Assertiveness

Once, on a walk with my young daughter and my old dog, we were confronted by a Rotteweiler who was so aggressive that he broke out of a glass window of his house to try and get to us. As any parent would do, I got between the Rottweiler and my "pack" and shouted him off. We all have a fighter in us that can be called out when necessary. The problem is when we take too long to find that fighter.

Sometimes the reason for an untenable situation lies in a conditioned response to not fight. We are admonished by our culture to not fight. Fighting is wrong. Anger is bad. We must travel the path of acceptance. While admirable, these ideas can be overplayed and dull effective responses. Taking a more muscular and vigorous response is often the key to tap into our greater resources.

In the world of corporate purchasing, there are robust strategies in place to get the best prices from suppliers. Many of these strategies emphasize "win-win" when they really mean "you give now and you might get something later." These well-crafted "win-win" strategies are often designed to get what others want and to salve your "ego-ego." Purchasing agents may also insist that "all communication must go through purchasing." These are lousy rules for suppliers and are intended to put them in a submissive position. Are you allowing the rules of others to dictate your responses? To what extent have the traditional approaches of "getting along" or "compromise" actually made a situation worse?

The vast majority of people I work with could probably boost their assertiveness by 20 percent, 40 percent, or even 80 percent and still come across as quite accommodating, nice people—and be 200 percent more effective.

Muscles are activated by neurons firing. Often when people get back in the gym after a hiatus, they feel weak. Yet after just a few workouts, they start to feel stronger. This is not because their muscles have grown in such a short period. The reason is because the neural pathways are more efficient. The neural stimulation is of better quality so the muscle is working more efficiently. Future strength gains will come from actual muscular growth, but the initial improvements can mostly be described as coming from neural rehearsal. The phenomenon may also be called *remembering*.

By remembering our strengths, we can reinvigorate ourselves and have better responses to our challenges. The key is remembering our strengths, that we can be a fighter, and that we have the resources to handle the situation.

The common advice is not to live the past. My suggestion is to make frequent, positive visits. We should frequently return to our successes, our accomplishments, and achievements. These visits can be extremely restorative and immediately applicable to situations being faced today. A successful past is a lousy place to stay but an excellent place to visit.

These visits contain fuel to move forward proactively. If you have seen a boxing match, you have seen a boxer "cover up" defensively under a flurry of punches. The proper strategy is to cover up and then time a counterpunch. Too often people "cover up" but forget to counter. Their reaction is to just "cover and cover" versus "cover and counter." A permanent defense is a de facto retreat.

A business owner cannot cover their ears to complaints about poor behavior of a team member. Management cannot cover their eyes to possible ethical lapses even from top producers and rainmakers. A football team cannot win with a great defense. They need at least some offense to show up. We need to press forward and not look for exits. We need to remember the benefits of offense.

Assertiveness is a habit best displayed daily. The saying goes "time flies when you're having fun." And yet it is equally true that time flies by when we don't assert ourselves effectively. Time can get wasted on untenable situations when we don't take daily assertive steps.

Why wait for the right time when the right time can be now? Why wait for the right person when that person can be us? Why wait for the conditions to change when we can change the conditions? People hold themselves back by thinking someday they will be good enough. People wait for someday when today is the only day we ever have.

Look at how much admiration we have for people acting "heroically": a local team raising money for causes, a veteran continuing to create a nice life for the family despite horrific war wounds, or the professional acting with daily grace and hard work despite a debilitating illness. We admire these qualities. We also have these qualities and don't need to have a large barrier or adversity to act more assertively, right now.

Your assertiveness might just be what is needed now. You might just be the right person at the right time.

Daily assertiveness can be as simple as saying you don't see the reason for a "strategic initiative" when all the other heads are nodding agreement around a conference table. Daily assertiveness can show when speaking up when something needs to be said. Daily assertiveness can be swimming upstream when everyone else is going with the flow. Just like "someday island" is an awful place for a vacation, waiting for "someday" to be bold, assertive, or fully yourself is an awful habit.

Daily assertiveness means shifting to a more muscular stance—one where you are ready to take a problem head on. In karate, they have a stance called the "ready stance." Physically, it is just standing with arms to the side, feet apart, and weight slightly on the toes. Mentally, it is "primed for action." The stance is not an active combat stance, but simply being ready for action and primed to move with intent and force. We need to make efforts to get to that zone: primed and ready to get at it in a highly impactful way.

In 2015, passengers on a train bound for Paris (including three off-duty U.S. soldiers) subdued a man armed with an assault rifle with 270 rounds of ammunition, a pistol, and a knife. Their quick thinking certainly prevented a potential enormous tragedy for the other 500 passengers onboard. Whatever your untenable situation, keep your head on a swivel and be ready to take things on, whatever it may be.

Tips to be more of a fighter

- Challenge yourself to add incredible value today (in relationships, business, or team).
- See yourself as TRPATRT (The Right Person At The Right Time).
- Stay primed for action with your head on a swivel for risks and opportunities.
- Be the daily hero, not the daily victim.

Defining Standards

Many people carry around the untenable situations they have because their standards are too low.

Low standards are not necessarily global. A person may have extremely high standards related to work, but have very low standards for their health. Several doctors told my grandfather to just go home and live with the excruciating knee pain he developed in his late eighties. Doctor after doctor refused to treat him because people of his age often have bad health that would prohibit surgery and rehabilitation. My grandfather's health at the time was above the standard and his standard (which he insisted on until his death) was high personal mobility, even if it meant surgery, rehab, and the use of a wheeled walker. His standard in that area was quite high. He refused to let the standards of others limit his choices.

Some people have extremely high standards for the food they eat. Some people (including yours truly) have treated their stomach like a garbage can. Over time, if that low standard is maintained, it can lead to serious issues.

A standard is the minimum acceptable limit for a particular domain. In metals, purity is described by the number of "nines." A metal that is 99 percent pure is called "two nines." A higher standard maybe "five nines" (99.999 percent pure) or even "six nines" (99.9999 percent pure). Some manufacturing applications require the higher standards in order to ensure the quality of their products.

Are your standards meeting the performance required? Are you applying "two nines" to a "six nines" situation?

Restaurants in California receive letter grades from the health inspector that are posted prominently for customers to see. Would you eat a place with a bad grade? Unlikely. Why then do we tolerate lower standards in other parts of our lives?

In recent news, many organizations are in turmoil because men in positions of power are alleged to have abused that power and sexually harassed female employees. What was the standard of those men's peers and the board members who heard the rumors but practiced an informed lack of curiosity? Their standard was likely "as long as the person is making the company money" all is good. They had high standards for performance and low standards for how people are treated.

Uncover your unrecognized standards. People often do not realize they have (or need) standards until a choice is made or a line has been crossed. Do yourself and others the favor of being conscious of your own standards. Consider people that "just want a job" then are unhappy with the job they find; they had unrecognized standards they did not honor. Don't settle, select. Review the list below. Are there standards that you feel you should be more assertive about? Are there standards that relate to your untenable situation?

- Performance standards (for self and others)
- "Pure enjoyment" standards (time and quality of play or hobby experiences)
- Career standards (job or function you will accept)
- Income standards
- Learning and enrichment standards (quality and amount of time for personal development)

- Nutritional standards (quality and timing of nutrition consumed)
- Relationship standards
- Peer standards (who you will consider your peers and with whom you aspire to be a peer)
- Health standards (including amount of mobility, time spent on...)
- Environmental standards (places you will stay or live)
- Amount of art/creativity in your life
- Amount of new and productive stimulation (entertainment, plays, music...)
- Moral standards (standards related to your guiding principles)
- Altruistic standards (time and resource standards related to the betterment of others)

After getting clear on standards (and raising those standards where appropriate), it is critical to be clear on possible approaches to maintain those standards. Too many people do not realize the breadth of behavioral styles available to them. They end up using strategies that they are comfortable with, but which might not be appropriate to the situation. They diagnose the situation poorly and end up curing badly.

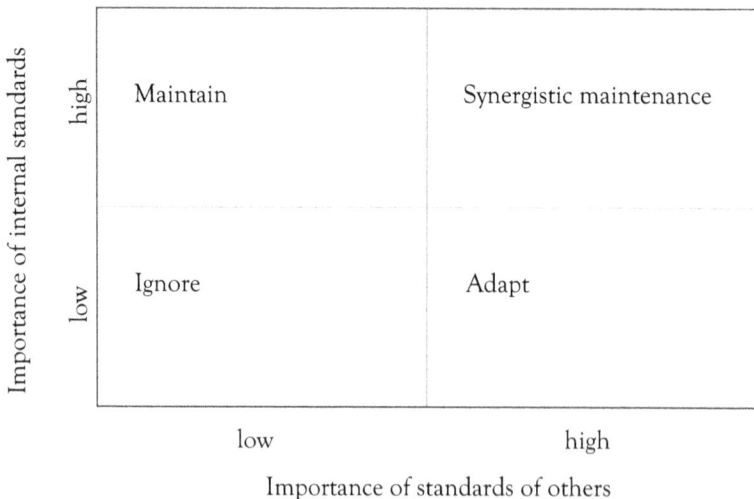

Figure 8.1 *Standard keeping*

Kenneth Thomas and Ralph Kilmann identified five basic ways people might react to conflict: they can stand up for things that are important to them, they can accommodate others, they might avoid the situation altogether, they might compromise, or they might collaborate. People can have a preferred approach. Problems occur when a person's preferences are a mis-match for the situation at hand. When we chart the importance of our standards to the importance of the standards of others (see Figure 8.1), it looks like this:

- When our internal standards are high and the standards of others are low, we should not be shy about actively honoring those standards through strict maintenance (i.e., fight for it).
- When the standards of others are high, and our standards are low, we should graciously *adapt* (i.e., let others have their way).
- When no standards are readily apparent for any parties, the situation is best served by *avoiding* or ignoring (i.e., let it go).
- When our internal standards are high and the standards of others is high, then we should look for synergistic ways for each party to have their needs met (i.e., look for ways to meet both sets of needs).

The middle ground (not noted in the chart) is that area where standards are somewhat important to both parties and best served via a *compromise* (i.e., split the difference).

Too often people overrely on adapting or compromising. These approaches are not appropriate when our standards are high. We can adapt or compromise on preferences like where we go to eat with a group. We can accommodate a salad sometimes even though I might prefer a burger. No biggie. However, we cannot be wishy-washy on ethical standards like how employees are treated or travel expenses are accounted for.

Are your approaches in alignment with your standards? Too often people stick with one approach when they could use a variety of approaches. Too many people adapt when they should be more cognizant of (and champions for) their own standards. Find the appropriate way to maintain your standards in the healthiest way possible—do not feel obligated to adapt when the situation calls for a more assertive response.

Making a Stand

Untenable situations also happen because we turn our back and "run." Running might be avoiding situations. Running might be changing locales or jobs. In the popular *Game of Thrones* series, Jon's father, Ned, instructs him that a soldier has ceased to be a soldier when he turns and runs. His heart is lost and most of their danger to others is gone.

How many people can you think of that did not make progress because they flitted from thing to thing or abandoned something when it got hard?

Free divers are exceptionally good at being uncomfortable. They can dive to tremendous depths and for surprising durations. Part of the trick is building up a tolerance to carbon dioxide. Oddly, it is not the need for oxygen but the need to get rid of CO_2 that causes people to be uncomfortable. It is a good survival response, but dive times (of experienced people) can be extended by managing it. For these divers, the training involves developing a tolerance to the buildup of carbon dioxide. They can get used to being uncomfortable.

Just because a person is uncomfortable does not mean they are in the wrong place.

Making a stand means finding your cause and not just moving because the situation is uncomfortable. The military uses the phrase "embrace the suck." It may be a crude phrase, but it makes a good point. But the point is not just soldiering on whenever anything is hard. The key is to practice the enlightened version of "embracing the suck." Don't embrace the suck of others but rather endure the tough stuff that *you* choose for your own growth and enjoyment.

Some people mistakenly think that any hard time is a good development opportunity. Other people mistakenly think hard times should be avoided. Neither way of thinking is healthy. The key is embracing those things that are our choice and not the choice of others. All sucks are not created equal. Making a stand has an additional benefit of helping us address major flaws (e.g., time management, assertiveness, etc.) and let us work on higher level issues. It is the difference in being a work in refinement or a work in progress. A work in refinement is when a person is consistently building on skills. A work in progress is when a person continues to struggle with the basics.

Many worthwhile things require a healthy sacrifice (effort, energy, stamina). They do not require the sacrifice of your ideals, values, or self-worth. Healthy sacrifices will actually enhance those aspects. The temptation may be to seek greener pastures, but don't give up on your plot just yet. That gook on your boots might be the fertilizer.

The Overplayed Helpful

There's a common problem with most ideas about strengths in that they are commonly described one-dimensionally. A person is frank. A person is diplomatic. The truth is that many strengths are best displayed two-dimensionally or in complement with another strength. A person who is frank (can give the news) and who is also diplomatic (says things in a way people can hear them) is much more effective than the frank person being more frank or the diplomatic person being more diplomatic.

This concept, called Paradox Theory, was developed by Dr. Dan Harrison and also applies to helpfulness. Helpfulness requires the complimentary effective trait of assertiveness. Assertiveness is taking care of one's own interests. Alan Weiss (author of numerous books including *Lifestorming* and *Thrive*) is known for his admonishment to "put on your own oxygen mask first." He is referring to the instructions commercial airlines give to put on your own oxygen mask before trying to help others sitting beside you like small children. We can best help others if we help ourselves first. The overplayed helpful is that person who tries to help too much without proper attention to their own needs. This often leads to feeling overwhelmed and may impact other areas of a person's life. Prolonged, the person may start to have feelings of resentment and being taken advantage of. Sometimes this can be seen with caregivers to their parents or other family members with long-term care needs. Sometimes these family members after repeated giving get tired and may turn resentful.

A sharp edge helps a knife do its job correctly. A dulled knife is actually quite dangerous. It requires the use of more force than necessary and is awkward to use. A sharp knife cuts cleanly without excessive force. People need an edge too. Being an overly helpful person dulls our edge. We can be an appeaser, but when our own priorities get squashed or subverted or ignored, the tension builds up. Being overly helpful puts people at risk of losing out in the short term, then getting frustrated, angry, and paradoxically may become more demanding as their frustrations mount.

I have seen many leaders in organizations get tripped up by the need to be helpful. A new leader who used to do the same job of those he is now managing might have this problem. He may be tempted to jump back into the old functions and help people do the job he used to do. In select situations, it might be perfectly appropriate to go back and help as a backup for people, but then larger picture things might not get addressed.

If there's a new process someone needs to learn, a leader might need to do more hand-holding or actually show people how to do something, but that should be the exception and not the rule.

Is your rule to help everyone else first? Is your second rule to try to be even more helpful win the first rule is not working? Do you then feel exhausted? Angry? Resentful? It is an unsustainable (can I say untenable) habit?

Being an overly helpful person has its limits. A leader I know was asking for help on his vision for the company. When he was having trouble articulating the vision to me, it was apparent he was trying to create the vision all on his own. I told him he needed to include his team. What is he protecting his team from? He wanted to give them all the answers.

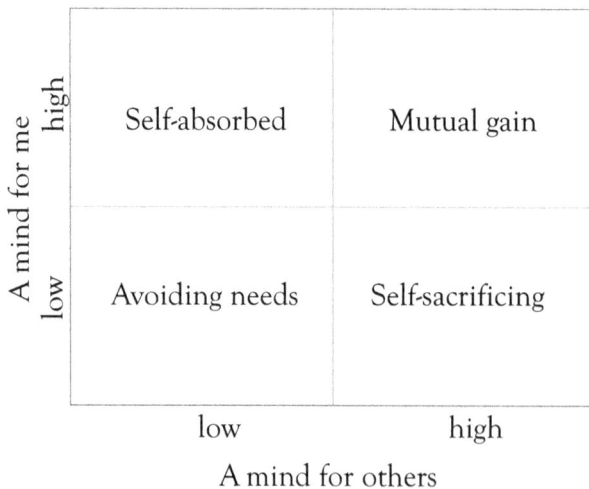

Figure 8.2 Overplayed helpful

He had a misplaced idea that the best way to help was to do all the heavy lifting for them. Ironically, his team would actually have preferred to give their input on the vision. He was not doing them any favors. Being too helpful can have a negative impact on others.

What is often overlooked is that your helpful may not actually be helpful. Your helpful might be stifling and perceived as if meddling by others. The key is balance: taking care of your own needs while being aware of the needs of others.

Consider the dynamic of a *mind for me* versus *mind for others* in Figure 8.2 above. It is based on work done by Dr. Dan Harrison on traits related to work preferences. While Dr. Harrison shows the connection between assertiveness and helpful, I find it easy for people to consider in terms of having a mind for their own interests compared to having a mind for other people's interests. A person who is all about their own needs and ignores the needs of others is just self-absorbed and likely to dominate needs of others. Self-absorption is isolating and it is a nonstarter in working with others. The person who considers the needs of others out of proportion to their own needs can fall into the self-sacrificing trap. This person might also be wrapping themselves in the cocoon of the martyr.

Martin Seligman (widely considered the founder of positive psychology and author of *Authentic Happiness*) is famous for identifying and helping people overcome "learned helplessness." He posits that through conditioned responses, people can get habits that keep them feeling defeated and in a helpless state.

A strong case can be made for the existence of "learned overhelpfulness." There are several reasons people may have learned to be overhelpful:

- Culture (e.g., The southern United States's high value for "nice")
- A need to be liked
- A habit of putting others first
- Inculcated with ideals of humility

With a prolonged habit of overhelpfulness, people can lose their sense of assertiveness. Losing the sense of assertiveness is like losing one of the primary senses. Loss of a primary sense is usually the result of an accident or birth defect. It is rarely the result of a voluntary action. The senses are too valuable. Yet people give up their sense of assertiveness all the time.

- They are overly accommodating others.
- They want to get along at any cost.
- They do not feel like they should have an opinion.
- They feel their preferences are superficial and not really important.

These layers add up. For many people who are habitual overhelpers, these layers cover them up like a kid bundled up for winter, so thick with layers of coats, sweaters, shirts, and hats that they can have barely move. The image is cute for kids, but it is sad to think of a grown person muffled up like that. It inhibits the range of motion. It slows down response time. It makes it easy to stumble. It is stifling.

How often have you

- taken on a project for another when you really wanted to say no?
- decided to finish something for someone when they did it incorrectly the first time (i.e., fixed their work for them)?
- said you have no preference for restaurant/movie/destination and then actually did not like the activity that was selected?
- let a habitually opinionated person sway you from your choice?
- felt taken advantage of for help you offered?
- shrank back from asking for what you wanted or needed?

If your answers were more "rare" or "never," you might want to take a deeper look at your degree of helpfulness. Even the Mother Teresa's of the world (extremely giving and generous people) can draw sharp lines about what they will or will not do. Mother Teresa was not known to be a pushover. Clarity is a gift. Staying clear on what you want and need is an essential part of maximizing your ability to help others.

Many leaders I work with have this problem. They try too hard. They paint on other people's canvases. This is especially evident during performance review time. One leader I know was wondering how to get his COO to improve his department and to contribute to the annual growth of the organization. The leader even tried to get me to help. "What do you think he should do? His areas might just be more efficiency." My answer: "Ask him. That's his job."

If it feels like your situation with leading others is too hard, you are likely making it too hard. Let the responsibility lie where it belongs. You can't be on both sides of a teeter-totter and make it work. There needs to be weight and energy on both sides. Let others do their own lifting. Let other people solve their own problems.

Many leaders come to me saying they want to be better delegators, and their teams want it too. The key point is to shake off the need to be overly helpful. Often what is going on is that they are just being too darn helpful. It's not about delegation, which is a skill, but it's about being overly helpful, which is a damaging mind-set.

There are times and places to fight. We should be aware of and honor our standards and not always be ready to accommodate. If fighting never solved anything, what of cowardice?

Summary and Tips

- Realize that most people can be 50 percent more assertive and still be "nice" people.
- Find your buried preferences.
- Don't confuse nice with "must accommodate."
- Redefine "helpful" as "mutually helpful" (make sure there is a win-win for you too).
- Beware bad faith overtures of "win-win" designed to salve your "ego-ego."
- Uncover and raise your standards. Don't settle, select.
- Effectively enforce your standards in ways that are appropriate to the situation.
- Define yourself as a hero of circumstance, not a victim of circumstance.
- Vacation in the past to revisit your successes and reenervate your forgotten strengths.

- Don't wait to be a big hero; be a daily hero in small but incremental ways.
- Embrace hard things that you choose to endure, not the things imposed by others (i.e., embrace your own suck).
- Challenge damaging beliefs that cut off your sense of assertiveness.

CHAPTER 9

Being an Inner Alchemist: Creating Novel Solutions

- Why tinker when we can tackle?
- Making models
- Going kinetic
- Inspiration for your perspiration
- The alacrity formula

There are methods to create dramatically different conditions. The solution is often not a matter of more. The solution is often a matter of degree of difference. People can develop their own inner alchemy to access more moves than they ever imagined.

Why Tinker When We Can Tackle?

Many people waste time by tinkering instead of tackling. They fool themselves that more of the same will make a difference. The "fallacy of the more" comes into play, meaning the belief that more of the same will make a difference. In the oil industry, a drilling rig will drill vertically and then deep underground, it will make a sharp turn and drill horizontally. That turn is called the kickoff point and it is made because the oil industry learned horizontal wells produced much more than just drilling deeper vertical wells. Are you in need of a kickoff point? Will more of the same really get you the results that you want in the timeframe you desire?

People spend too much time nibbling around the edges of the issues instead of going to the heart of the matter. People need to get out of the tinkering business an into the tackling business.

When I was a kid, we played pickup games of football. I was not the best athlete on the field, but I found that even a skinny kid like me could knock people out of bounds and stop a play. What use is it to just keep up with someone who has the ball? Sometimes they gotta be stopped and a sharp right angle off the field changed everything.

People can wear themselves out by adapting to untenable situations in organizations. A colleague described the effect of all this adaptation as "organizational calluses." These can occur when the frictions between two groups or around an ineffective leader build up to protect the organization.

A person can develop calluses on their thinking by not addressing their problems directly. They tinker. They consider. They explain away. They do everything but getting to the root cause and addressing the key issue with high energy.

We need to change our thinking and realize there are likely many ways to address an issue once it is identified. We have unlimited creativity, but limited energy. Energy can get frittered away on everything around the issue instead of concentrating creative energies at the issue.

Below are some things to consider to get you into a tackling mode versus a tinkering mode.

Can you nullify the main impediment? If you go to the beach you will be aware of riptides. Riptides will pull even the strongest swimmers far from the shore. The way out of a riptide is not to fight the current. Lifeguards will advise people to swim parallel to the beach to get out. You likely do not need to do more, and likely need to do things decidedly different and stop fighting things that cannot be fought. An organization can sidestep a dominant competitor by redefining a market. A leader can work with the business units that want to collaborate instead of wasting efforts with those that do not want to. A person can replace a bad habit with a new good habit instead of just relying on will power to avoid the bad habit.

Can you think bigger? For example, if declining sales is an issue, maybe more of the existing sales training is not the answer. Instead, perhaps consider how best to attract key decision makers. More of the same training might just make salespeople more efficient at talking to non-decision makers. It would likely be more valuable if salespeople were more effective at contacting and relating to senior decision makers.

Can you fix or solve this issue instead of adapting to it? What is the true heart of the matter? In business, the main impediment might be too many priorities, or lack of credibility in a new market, or lack of experienced talent. Actions that seek to mitigate the effects are a lot less useful than ones that eliminate it. Consider the tactic of "robo-calling" as a marketing tool. Robo-calling tinkers around the edges of trying to make effective sales actions. The real problem is that people do not answer the phone anymore because of the onslaught of scammers and marketers. Robo-calling requires enormous energy. It takes thousands of calls to reach a single person who might buy. It's not lazy, but it's certainly not smart.

Counterintuitively, the more time we spend tinkering with issues the more energy it takes. Tackling gets to the heart of the matter and is decisive action to improve conditions. Tinkering draws things out even though it seems easier at the time.

On Adapting

In *The New Rational Manager*, Kepner and Tregoe highlight that any given issue can be addressed in one of four actions: corrective, preventive, contingent, or adaptive.

Corrective actions fix causes from the past. Preventive actions remove causes in the future. Contingent actions mitigate possible effects in the future. Adaptive actions help a person deal with the effects today.

If a person has a throat infection, the corrective action is to take antibiotics. The preventive actions might include washing hands regularly and avoiding known sick people. Contingent actions might include staying at home and resting. Adaptive actions might include "powering through" like nothing ever happened.

My brother had an awful car in high school that required someone (usually me) to hold open the carburetor in cold weather to start. He would have liked to fix it, but luckily labor (me) was cheap and it was not so bad, so we adapted.

For cars and colds, adaptive action may be appropriate. The trouble is that adaptation does not work when things are intolerable or within a person's control to fix. It's the wrong approach for the situation.

In the southwestern United States, skin cancer is a big concern. The many beautiful days of sunshine and pleasant weather are a risk factor for many, especially those with fair skin or bald heads (I have both). The corrective action for skin cancer is straightforward and unpleasant: surgery, chemotherapy, and radiation. Preventive actions include limiting exposure and regular screenings. Contingent actions might include intensified rounds of chemo or radiation. Adaptive action would be to live with it. In that case, the adaptive action might come with heavy doses of morphine or checking into hospice.

In the example above, most people would not choose adaptive action unless all the other courses of action had been tried. Why? The costs are too high. Yet for many, dealing with other non-life-threatening issue, they default to adaptive action, when they should be eliminating the cause, preventing a possible re-occurrence, or preparing future steps to ameliorate the effects.

There is nothing wrong with adaptive action. There are many times when it is the perfectly appropriate course of action. I inherited a dog when my grandfather passed away. I was not in the market for another dog, but we agreed to take it. Pepper was excellent for my grandfather. She is quiet, generally calm, and followed him everywhere in the house. As the new male in her life, she now follows me everywhere in the house. She gets anxious if she cannot see me or does not know where I am. It is a little unnerving to have something staring at you all the time, but I've adapted and it works ok. Corrective action would be to get rid of the dog, but it has not gotten to that point yet (figure 9.1).

The point is not to overplay adaptive action. If the accumulating costs exceed the costs to move, then it would be wise to get moving.

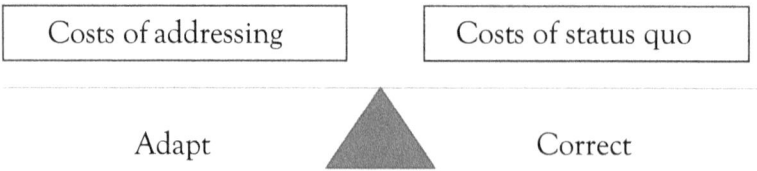

Costs of addressing	Costs of status quo
Adapt	Correct

Figure 9.1 *Adapt or correct*

Creating Models

Creating models can help a person get the best out of themselves. What are the primary factors that contribute to 80 percent of your success? The answer to that question is a model you can use to boost effectiveness. Put another way, if you can distill that formula that drives you to be your best, you have a potent prescription for success. For each person, there are a few key factors that, if present to a significant degree, can catapult their success. These factors can be uncovered by answering two questions:

- What does it look like when I am at my best?
- What are the key factors that contribute to that success?

Let's look at two examples.

Casey is a senior leader tasked primarily with business development. He has a great track record of success in building new territories and the emerging leaders that will support those territories. When he is at his best he is

- moving at a fast pace;
- spending considerable face time with clients;
- actively engaged in the coaching and mentorship of emerging leaders;
- collaborating with his team and other senior leaders on ways to drive revenue; and
- networking in the business and philanthropic community.

What are some of the factors contributing to that success?

- Working on visible, financial results (being able to show tangible impacts on the business)
- Significant face time with people (sociability and collaboration)
- Opportunity to impact the development of future leaders (people interest)
- Moving *quickly* (quick tempo)
- Having variety in activities, locations, and people

- Opportunity to help the community (altruism)
- Being able to create his own plans and to execute on them (leadership and autonomy)

The more that Casey can integrate factors like business impact, recognition, moving quickly, team environment, variety, autonomy, people development, and altruism, the better his performance will be.

Let's look at another example. Sharon is a senior operations leader and responsible for managing major new initiatives across the organization. She works with a variety of stakeholders to make sure their needs are met and that all the details related to business systems (finance, quality, IT, etc.) are addressed. She thrives in an environment presenting progress to senior executives, pushing for task completion, keeping many people on task even when they do not report to her, and making sense of details. She is the type of person that likes taking on a project and seeing it to the finish line.

Sharon success factors may be:

- Recognition
- Planning and organizing
- Working in a team environment
- Working in an environment with little ambiguity (mission-focused)
- Working on details

If Casey or Sharon did not have the above factors to a significant degree, their effectiveness would likely be impacted. If they have those things, then they will likely be the proverbially happy and effective camper. The presence or absence of these factors has a potent triggering effect. Imagine a world in which Casey had little control of his plans, was not working on revenue generating activities, and had little social or community contact. That would be a terrible situation for him. Imagine a world in which Sharon was working in an environment of high ambiguity or one in which she was not being asked to make changes, just maintain current systems. Neither would likely perform very well.

Each of us has their own performance triggers. The more of these performance triggers we have firing at the same time the better.

We all have our performance triggers that can be refined to help us work at our best. But everyone is different, so what works best for one may not work for you. Let's try and find what works best for you.

Step 1: Describe a couple instances when you were at your best. This may be at work or other scenarios. What are you doing? When are you doing it? Who were you with?

Step 2: Why do you think you perform at your best? What are some of the biggest contributing factors? Were you by yourself? Were you with others? What kinds of projects where you working on?

Step 3: Evaluate your results. What parts of the model can be replicated on a regular basis?

Here are a potential list of performance triggers to get you thinking. These performance triggers will help you build models that will help you perform more effectively. Performance triggers can include the environment we work in and time spent on certain activities that reflect our highest values.

- Team environment
- High autonomy environment
- For-profit or nonprofit environments
- Working from home or working in a formal office
- Time spent on hobby or sports
- Time spent with friends and family
- Time spent at church or community activities
- Time for philanthropy
- Time spent mentoring or teaching others
- Time spent in creative pursuits (art, writing, or performance)
- Financial pursuits
- Being productive in the yard or around the house
- Travel
- Reading
- Exercise
- Learning something new
- Getting things knocked off a list
- Working alone
- Working with others in a team environment

- Working under tight deadlines
- Working behind the scenes or in a support role
- Being out in front of people (i.e., leading or speaking)
- Prestige/status/recognition
- Ability to bring big thinking and ideas to the table
- Being in a decision-making role

Maximize the top things that trigger high performance in you and minimize those things that do not add to your performance. Top sales people are often positively triggered by attaining financial goals, working autonomously, having their results be recognized, and by working at a high tempo. If they are asked to take on a sales management role, some may struggle because they do not have the same amount of positive triggers. The new role may require people development, management of systems made by others, and less direct impact on top line revenue. For some, that lack of positive triggers explains why they cannot make the transition. It seems like a simple thing to work most on things that we enjoy. Yet many people forget and try to adapt a formula for success that does not fit them at all.

Going Kinetic

It's not all in your head. The modern work of business and organizations is mostly a mental game, but it is not all played between our ears. While people might highlight the need for the right mind-set or applying emotional intelligence to work effectively, the advice overlooks key possible causes of poor performance that are rooted in the physical world.

I can tell you from great experience that it is very hard for someone to be more open, patient, listening, creative, discerning or otherwise effective when they are exhausted, underexercised, suffer from limited range of motion, and they are fueling primarily through their caffeine delivery vehicle of choice. People make awful nutrition choices. People have awful mobility habits that induce pain and a sclerotic physicality. That's a fancy way of saying we sit too much; most people spend way too much time at their desk or on a plane. If those habits are the cause, then no amount of positive thinking will be the cure.

I recommend people get kinetic both metaphorically and in reality. Going kinetic is a phrase from the military meaning active engagement. It means getting into motion. When the military goes kinetic, things are going to happen. When a person goes kinetic, big things can happen too.

A body is basically a device to carry a brain around. Is yours in good shape and contributing to the mental game or taking away from it? There are many studies (including studies on students and grades) suggesting that there is a powerful performance benefit from exercise and movement. The smart kids seem to get it. What about you?

How to Put Kinetic to Work for You

- Define and establish performance habits that involve basic movement. You don't need to train like a Navy SEAL operator, but a person does need basic cardio fitness, strength, and mobility and habits that address each.
- Define and established performance habits related to nutrition. This includes hydration. Give yourself permission to eat and fuel. Do not feel constrained by schedules or preferences of others. Have good quick snacks around and plan a day that includes meals.
- Define and establish performance habits related to sleep. Figure out when you are going to stop looking at that phone and transition to some rest.
- Find one or two things to do that will make a physical improvement in your environment. Scrap that pile of magazines waiting to be read. Clean your desk or the desktop of your computer. Whatever it is pick something quick and straightforward and make progress on that immediately.
- Live out a metaphor. For many working professionals, the impact of their efforts are not readily visible. Organized races, group events, and even personal challenges in the gym or on a track are powerful metaphors and physical expressions of wins. Give yourself the opportunity to display your own grit, strengths, and will in tangible ways.

- Use perspiration for your inspiration. Feeling better is one thing, but there are plenty of studies that show that exercise can also boost creativity. How many times have some ideas or insights come to you while out and about on a jog or doing some other light cardio? The endorphins are certainly at work (and those make us happier), but there are also other chemicals that are generated during exercise that can make people more creative.

- Be aware of timing. Everybody has their own times where their energy is highest or they are best able to focus. Some people work best in the morning. Some people work best in the afternoons. Find those times that work best for particular activities. For example, I write best in the morning, so I schedule accordingly and try to put other rote tasks in the afternoon when I am not so creative.

The Alacrity Formula

While people talk about the important of speed, I believe *alacrity* is what people really need. As I have mentioned earlier in the book, alacrity is moving with both speed and enthusiasm.

All speed and no enthusiasm is just robotic. All enthusiasm and no speed is just cheerleading. We need both.

A = S + E

Alacrity is speed plus enthusiasm. Alacrity can create enormous shifts in productivity. The problem is that too many people focus on speed. They try to work out complicated time management regimes. These can help to a degree, but the rest of the improvement will come from working on enthusiasm.

But where does enthusiasm come from? Enthusiasm is not just being a high-energy person. Even-keeled people can be very enthusiastic, but just not be really expressive about it. Enthusiasm comes from working on things that are in alignment with a mission that is important to a person.

Missions are important because they represent important values in action. Activities that are not related to a compelling mission are just tasks. It is hard to execute well and consistently in the absence of excitement.

We can create mission statements that are broad like "My mission is to be a great provider for my family and create a loving environment where my family can thrive."

We can also create mission statements for a specific areas of our life like work or community. An example might be "to create enormous value for customers and create a work environment that people feel blessed to be a part of."

I make no suggestions on what a person's mission should be or what should be included, but I do suggest people have one. We all need to make sure our enthusiasm is high and stays high. Making mission statements is one way to do it.

Developing and Testing a Mission Statement

Briefly describe (in one or two sentences) why you do what you do. You can describe a mission statement that encompasses a big part of your life or you can make one focused on a specific aspect of your life like work. To test it, take out your mission statement and review regularly (daily or a couple times per week). Does it create a sense of enthusiasm and excitement? If not, then you may need to rethink it. Are the things on your calendar and to-do list strongly related to your mission? If not, that may explain plateaus in productivity.

Dr. Dan Harrison, the creator of the Harrison Workplace Inventory (and who I mentioned earlier in relation to his work on paradox theory) has also done research on enjoyment. His research shows that people that enjoy 75 percent of more of their work are three times more likely to be successful at it. Enjoyment and enthusiasm are closely related. If we want to maximize the odds of being successful, we must know what is exciting and enjoyable to us. Once we know, we can design work and career to maximize our impact. We can get busy (fast) doing things we don't enjoy much, but it will always take a lot of discipline and the results will likely not be great.

Alacrity is a function of speed and enthusiasm. We should be enthused about the destination, but we should also focus on these two critical aspects of speed. Get to it. Get done. Move on.

Birds have especially light bones. For many, the mass of their bones is lighter than the mass of their feathers. Down to their bones they are light. Working on alacrity makes us light and maneuverable and a great asset to those that want to fly high and perhaps whistle along the way.

Summary and Tips

- Consider more options than just adaptation to resolve issues. Use more tackling and less tinkering.
- Find your personal formula for you to be at your best. This can include the environments and activities and trigger your best expression of your strengths.
- Find more inner resources by maximizing your physical resources through the use of physical performance routines and nutrition.
- Boost your momentum by working with alacrity. Alacrity includes speed and enthusiasm. Analyze those factors that may be getting in the way of starting fast and stopping fast. Also look for ways to maximize and maintain enthusiasm.

CHAPTER 10

Going Public and Taking Action

- "It's fine" and other vulnerability patches
- From out of the woodwork: help
- Getting it out in the open: examples for leaders and organizations
- Putting it all together

Progress can be made on big issues in leadership and in organizations. Progress can be made when we are less guarded, ask for help, and take a structured approach to forming key steps. There is power in going public. The power of sunlight makes things look more manageable and opens up avenues of support and innovation.

It's Fine and Other Vulnerability Patches

Some might suggest that being vulnerable is some sort of choice, that we can somehow protect ourselves by being less vulnerable. Being vulnerable is a choice, but not in the way many people think.

Here, let's make a distinction between vulnerability and exposure. Everyone going through life is *exposed* to some level of risk. Whether someone chooses to be vulnerable or not, they are exposed to criticism, second guessing, blame, suspicion, failure, or some sort of harm. Exposure comes with the territory of life.

The truth is we are exposed whether we like it or not. People can observe us and for the most part are fairly cognizant of our failings. We may think that we are hiding something, but people are likely to know what it is or know that something is amiss.

I can manage

People can't help

I am fine

People don't understand

It doesn't matter

Issue

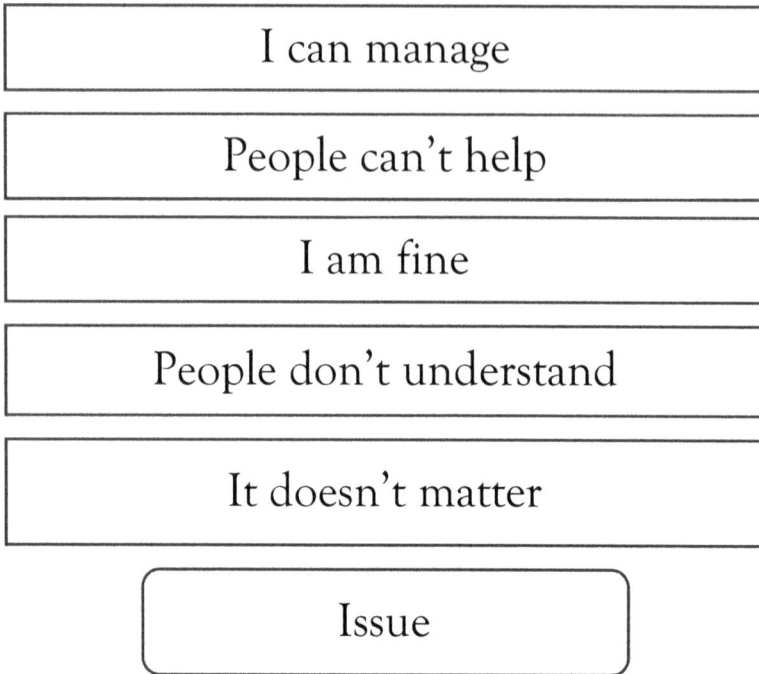

Figure 10.1 *Common vulnerability patches*

When hiking in Colorado, I noticed many of the descriptions in trail guides talked about the degree of exposure on a trail. They were not just describing the amount of shade on the trail. The guides were describing the degree to which there were sharp cliffs and drop-offs. We stayed off the trails with big exposures because I am scaredy-cat about heights. However, almost any trail has some degree of exposure. There are no risk-free steps. Exposure is part of the journey.

Our choice is to remain guarded or to let ourselves be vulnerable to take in appropriate information from the environment. The former feeds into inertia and misdirection, while the other offers a path forward.

Being guarded adds layers of illogic and pretense. It is a truism that a strong offense is a strong defense. I would also say that a strong defense is often covering a big pretense. Shifting to an unguarded mind-set does not change the degree of exposure but it does increase the range of options we have to alleviate the situation.

In an effort to reduce their feelings of exposure, people might try to apply patches like Microsoft puts security patches on their software vulnerabilities.

In the case of people (as highlighted in Figure 10.1), the patches add up layers of illogic that cover up the problem and keep people stuck.

Common Vulnerability Patches

- I can manage on my own—denial of the value of outside support.
- People can't help—denial of the interest of others to help.
- I am fine—denial of the lack of personal impact of the situation.
- People don't understand—denial of the validity of the perspective of others.
- It does not matter—denial of the importance of the situation.

There are medicines that work well to remove warts, but they work best when the thick dermal layers are removed first. Layers need to be stripped away to allow the medicine to get to the root of the problem. The degree to which we can remove the influence of these patches covering up perceived vulnerabilities, the quicker we can get the issue resolved.

Out of the Woodwork: Help

Have you ever had a big shock from seeing some kind of creepy crawly in your house? The creep factor seems especially strong when it is in the kitchen or the bedroom. But if we see the same critter outside, it does not seem to be as bad. If we saw that same cockroach, snake, or spider outside, it may not even raise our heartbeat at all. We might even be curious: "wow I never knew they made webs that big." Seeing things out in the light of day makes things much more manageable. If it works for spiders (or whatever provokes a negative response in you), then it can also work on some of our problems. It will not hurt and will likely make things look much easier to deal with.

Getting things out in the open has another key positive effect: it signals to others that there is an issue that they may be able to help with.

Horror films boost the fear factor by use of isolation. The characters are placed far out in the woods, in an empty hotel in winter in the Rocky Mountains, or in a spaceship that is light years from civilization. Isolation boosts fear. The fear factor can be reduced significantly if we know we are not alone.

I have noticed a funny dynamic with many of the people I have worked with over the years. While many of these people are very helpful, they are often very hesitant to ask others to help. Sometimes the reason is shame. More commonly, it is simply because asking for help did not occur to them. Don't let this be you. Do you want to help others? Most people do. Why then do we hesitate to reach out for help? Admission that there is a problem is a sign of strength, not weakness. And there are a multitude of resources out there that might speed resolution of your issue, if you allow it.

People can help in all sorts of ways if they know there is a need. People can help by sharing

- connections to others that may be beneficial;
- perspective to expand options or redefine the issue;
- direct advice and clear steps on how to handle;
- experience on how they have handled similar issues; and
- encouragement to keep going.

People can also be there to help with accountability. Once a plan has been made or next steps identified, it is always helpful to know there is someone else out there who will know if progress is being made or not.

People acting as sounding boards can also be extremely valuable. Sounding boards help by allowing a person to get out of their own head. How many times have we been able to get our own answer after voicing the question to another?

People can also help with observation. Just like a spotter helps when we are lifting a heavy barbell or a personal stylist can tell someone when something really works to enhance their appearance or not.

Look at the generosity on display for charitable drives for food, water, clothes, blood, and financial donations. People like to help.

I have a near involuntary Tourette-like twitch when it comes to people and their careers. It does not matter if we just met at a networking event or as part of an Uber ride, if there is a mention about careers or looking for work, I am immediately trying to see how I can help. I hate seeing people waste time in their job searches and I hate seeing employers wasting time by not having the right people. I do not think that I am alone in that inclination. Help will literally come out of the woodwork if we let it.

Rescue professionals have zero chance of helping someone if they cannot find them. They can have the will, the equipment, and the facilities to help, but that does not mean a thing if they cannot locate the person in need. That's why signaling devices like mirrors, lights, and whistles are such important components of an emergency pack. In an emergency, the degree to which you can help yourself through band-aids and other things will often pale in comparison with your ability to signal for help. We need to effectively signal when we need help.

Like moths to a flame, help will come if we flick on a light. You have no idea what is out there until you do. But that help needs to be drawn in and channeled. After people know there is a need, they need to know what it is that you are looking for. Simply telling people you need a job will just get you job offers that you may not be interested in. You need to be specific to help people help you.

Some tips on asking for help:

- Seek out those with no agenda beyond your own best interest. People with an axe to grind might be looking for a place to put said axe.
- Be specific about outcomes you want: a better organization, better relationships, or a better career.
- Save the history lesson. Limit the backstory to the pertinent facts and focus attention on where you want to go or want to see improvement.
- Show your effort. People that are seen to be trying to help themselves tend to attract the most help. Those perceived to be a big factor in their own helplessness tend to repel help.
- Be aware of the types of help beyond solving. See the list above for some ideas.
- Find those that have demonstrated success broadly or within the specific are you are concerned with.
- If confidentiality is important to you, do not request help from those that have gossiped to you about others.

- Do not feel compelled to take every piece of advice or perspective given. Some may not apply. Others may be a piece of the puzzle.
- Not all perspectives or help should be given equal weight. Give more credence to those sources of help that have the most experience.
- Thank people for their willingness to help even if the input given was not applicable in this context. There may be future contexts.

An odd but dangerous fact is that hikers suffering from dehydration and heat exhaustion will often separate themselves from their group. They will start to feel bad and sometimes wander off the trail away from others to rest under some shade. The disorientation makes them separate themselves from those who could best aid them, just when they need that help the most. we can fix many things on our own, but many situations will likely benefit from staying on the trail with a caring group of companions and not in self-imposed isolation.

Getting It Out in the Open: Examples for Leaders and Organizations

Leaders and organizations need to get things out in the open in order to deal with them effectively. Looking at specific conditions, behaviors, and assumptions that are likely untenable is a great place to start. Let's look at some examples and then describe a simple framework to help leaders identify their own specific opportunities and outline some steps to address.

Let's first look at some examples of untenable behaviors, conditions, and assumptions in the context of leadership:

Conditions

- Not having a ready replacement and hoping to be promoted
- Not being effective at people development, innovation, and strategy and expecting to contribute highly to the organization

- Not understanding the unique engagement factors of each of the people on your team
- Not being able to schedule four weeks ahead on your schedule

Behaviors

- Being rigidly inflexible
- Not being clear of accountabilities and holding people accountable
- Poor use of time
- Ineffective relating with senior leaders, peers, and direct reports
- Being a perfectionist
- Trying to be the smartest person in the room
- Confusing ridiculously busy with ridiculously productive
- Not effectively developing people so that they can be delegated to
- Too quick to give up time on their calendar
- Not helping organization avoid unintended consequences of initiatives
- Not taking appropriate care of physical and emotional health
- Trying to please everyone
- Being stuck in the tactical and expecting to impact the strategic

Premises

- Having to be the answer man/woman
- Expecting self and others to change overnight
- Expecting to change the behavior of a supervisor significantly
- Belief that a person can motivate another person
- Expecting people to know what to do without telling them
- Expecting people to make significant growth without having been involved in the goal-setting process
- Expecting a sink or swim approach to people development to not be expensive

While it might be tempting to just select from a list like the one above, it is good to take a more structured approach and one that is tailored to your own situation. Bicycles come in various standard size frames, but if you want to maximize performance, you will have a seat and handlebars adjusted for your unique proportions and preferences. The better the fit, the farther and faster a person can go.

First, let's look at two potential sources of information for development: environmental and self-reflective.

Environmental sources: Data from environmental sources is the equivalent of the check engine light. A leader can and should be paying attention to regular feedback from the environment. This can come in the form of formal 360 reviews of the leader, regular performance reviews, and one-on-one conversations with a leader's supervisors and their own direct reports. This source of information can provide good data points because (1) potential issues may be unrecognized by the leader and (2) the issue was important enough to be raised by people. Leaders might get feedback on behaviors or actions that affect a wide variety of people in the organization. This feedback might help a leader to see if there are specific areas of the organization that may benefit from a different approach like with senior leaders, peers in another business unit, or within their own team.

Self-reflective sources: A leader can get these through formal assessments that can highlight styles and preferences.

These two sources of information will highlight many potential areas a person could address to improve. The key is to find the top priorities to work on. A mistake that many leaders make is just looking at a list of 10 possible de-railing habits and then just pick 8 or 10. They need to be more discerning. Don't make the mistake of looking at lists and just thinking of them as a menu of options from which to choose. It is best to add some context to the goal so that the issues and priorities come out clearly. The best practice is to think about the destination and highlight critical issues and look from a more strategic perspective. The strategic way is much more effective because it keeps people out of the weeds and only trying to fix theoretical shortcomings. If we are going to work on issues doesn't it make sense to work on those that are most germane to the issues that are central and important to us? We do not want to think of leadership development as checking a list, or picking from a menu or like trying to get all the merit badges to get to the next level of a scout. Considering their own development is one of the most strategic things a leader can do.

Here are the steps to take:

Consider your B. If we are trying to figure out how to most effectively go from A to B, then we need to have a good understanding of B. To get to that in terms of leader effectiveness start by asking:

> What is my vision for myself as a leader in the next one to two years? What are the issues that I am resolving? What kind of team do I have? In what ways do I expect to be contributing?

Get real on A. The next step is to look at the current condition relative to the future condition. Ask yourself:

> If B is where I want to go, what does A look like now? What are the relevant aspects of my starting point?

Get real on critical issues. This step will surface those key issues that need to be addressed, considered, or resolved in order to achieve B.

Let's look at two examples, one for an emerging leader and one for a senior leader.

Emerging leader. In the first step, an emerging leader might identify they would like to be a more effective supervisor of the quality assurance team. In the second step, the leader might describe their current state as having strong technical skills, good familiarity with the strengths and weaknesses of members of the team, and some good fundamentals on the how to manage people in the day-to-day aspects of the work. In identifying critical issues, the leader might highlight the fact that the operation will be going through significant changes in terms of how the plant will operate (with new information systems and automation coming online) and that in addition to those changes they will be working with customers that have growing demands for sophistication for their suppliers. Based on those critical issues the leader would likely want to focus attention on the ability to develop people over time as well as the ability to clearly communicate with senior leaders and his direct reports.

Senior leader. As part of the first step, a senior leader might highlight that they would like to be able to lead more coherent innovation efforts. The leader might describe the current condition as one in which there are lots of ideas from direct reports (and many are encouraged and given the green light), but the efforts appear to be uncoordinated with other parts of the organization and seem to hit snags that hamper implementation. That leader might highlight critical issues as the need to be able to more affectively screen ideas in and out as well as more effective actions to ensure implementation.

Any of the issues highlighted in the gap between B and A are untenable if they are not addressed. One cannot say they want the result but are not willing to address the real issues with energy and focus.

After the critical issues are highlighted, then one must take steps to inoculate against inaction. Recall the diagram introduced in Chapter 1. This diagram explains why people may not take action even if there is an opportunity to improve a condition. All three elements (conviction, discipline, and aptitude) must be in place for people to address untenable situations.

Check your convictions. Are you sufficiently convinced that these are changes that are worth your time and attention?

Evaluate your aptitude. Do you know how you will address these issues? If not, what resources are there (mentorship, coaching, classes, training, books, etc.) can you access that will help you?

Assess your discipline. Do you have it in you to stick with it? If not, what structures can you put in place that will help you stay with it?

Additionally, be sure to:

Set measures. Set some measures that indicate progress. These measures may be quantifiable outcomes or they may be qualitative like more feelings of confidence. Be sure to schedule regular check-ins on progress and include use to people besides yourself to add additional layers of accountability.

Schedule a repeat of the evaluation steps of going from A to B and the critical issues. Conditions inside the organization change frequently. Conditions in the environment change frequently. The underlying need may have changed, leadership members may have changed, and business dynamics may have changed. It is critical to keep these things fresh and updated regularly.

In the context of organizations...

The process outlined above can also be used to uncover untenable behaviors, premises, and conditions that can affect the ability to achieve organizational goals. These may also come to light as an organization goes through a strategy process or a strategy refresh.

Let's take the example of a company with healthy business, but with concerns about their future talent. In the next three to five years, they are projecting a significant number of senior and middle managers will be retiring. The organization wants to be prepared for the transition. If they stay on the current path, there will be big concerns about the ability of the company to continue smooth operations and maintain safety.

Currently, the company has good talent, but they have also observed that some very promising emerging leaders left the company unexpectedly. Leadership has identified critical issues to include:

- No formal resources for training
- Emerging leaders are just expected to "get it" and supervisors (with few exceptions) do not take an active role in the development of their people.

These key issues (and perhaps others) must be addressed if the organization wants to have the leadership bench required to succeed in the future. The organization's leadership has been aware of these issues for some time, but cannot seem to get to the point of taking effective action. Why is that? The answers may be found by looking at the three factors of conviction, discipline, and aptitude.

This organization might have an issue around *conviction* if the right people or not enough of the right people are convinced on the need to address the talent issue and that it is their responsibility to take some action

This organization might have an issue around *discipline* if the parts of the organization that are expected to take an active role in mentoring are not doing so and their supervisors are also not being held accountable.

The organization might have an issue around *aptitude* if the leaders expected to mentor and develop emerging leaders don't know how to make plans and coach people over time or cannot do it very well.

Of course, the issue may also be a combination of weakness of one or more of the above factors and not just one. Leaders do need to regularly step back and take a strategic view to highlight critical issues that need to be addressed to get to their goals and then also be laser-focused on why they are stuck in place and not taking the logical steps to improve their condition.

Below are some examples of untenable situations for organizations:

- Being stingy on improvements, not just frugal on expenses (an organization cannot cut way to success)
- Being able to see new opportunities with people that do not have the experience or aptitude (for example, Kodak chemical engineers being expected to lead the way to a new digital future they may not be prepared for)
- Expecting business units to collaborate and synergize without leadership from the top (this one needs a healthy dose of intolerance)
- Deferring innovation efforts (the organizational equivalent of trying to time the stock market)
- Too many priorities (trying to ask too much of the organization at once)
- People incentivized at cross-purposes (expecting different business units and people to ignore how they are really recognized and compensated in the organization)

Organizations and their leaders have many issues they could improve. It is important to get real about what those big issues are and get to the heart of them.

Putting It All Together

Change for the better is a full time job.

—Adlai Stevenson

In this book I have described the makeup of untenable situations and why they are so important to address. Undesirable and worsening conditions need to be brought out and addressed assertively. Doing so will dramatically improve the enjoyment of our lives and our effectiveness at work.

In summary, there were nine points that were described to help people move forward:

Belief in self: We should always seek to bolster and support our trust in ourselves. There are the odd examples of people with an overblown estimation of their abilities. In professional settings, these are the exception and not the rule. Most people questions themselves too much and could boost their own self-belief by 2× and still be within the bounds of reality.

Vision: Vision provides direction and fuel for the road. Clarity of direction makes untenable thinking stand out clearly so we can take steps on those critical issues that stand between us and our desired future state. A powerful vision is also a source of excitement that keeps motivation high to assist through the rough patches.

Assertiveness: Similar to how people underestimate themselves, many people underassert themselves. They underutilize their assertiveness and mess up the timing. They are not assertive enough on the front-end and wind up having to compensate with harsher actions on the backend. Many people could be 2× more assertive and still be the pleasant, good, helpful people that they want to be.

Thinking different: Often, we can get into the trap that more of the same will help. Often we need to think differently. If we are on a treadmill, then running faster is no cure. We need to get off the treadmill and create games we can actually win.

Alacrity: Moving with speed and enthusiasm has amazing impact. We feel better, conditions start to improve, and momentum builds. There is amazing power in the starting fast, moving to completion of a task, and getting to the next thing. People can use that power to break out of unhelpful cycles and to prevent those cycles from repeating.

Getting real on costs: Untenable thinking involves not getting real on costs. We need to clearly see what not taking action to correct a problem is really costing us and those we care about.

Possibility thinking: We can get stuck because of poor premises that there is nothing that can be done to fix the situation. Just because we have not seen a solution yet does not mean that it doesn't exist. We can do much better by thinking about what can be done versus what cannot be done.

Perspective: People can get stymied because they look at the issue too broadly. They make little things appear bigger than they ought to be. They think a solution needs to fix all things instead of the few relevant things. It is important to breathe rationality of scope into our thinking. Things are often not as big or complicated as we make them out to be. When things are broken down into manageable chinks we can take the discrete steps that will materially improve the condition.

Vulnerability: It is essential for us to know that we don't have all the answers. There are many resources out there that can teach us how to do things or even how to think better about things. Patching our vulnerabilities can prevent us from accessing these things. Even self-reliance can be overplayed. It can prevent us from accessing valuable knowledge and from getting help from people who are more than willing to give it.

Continuous improvement is a process of maintenance. There is no final, permanently beautiful edifice. Every house (small or large) needs maintenance. Sometimes the need for maintenance is visible like an outdated kitchen or peeling exterior paint. Sometimes the maintenance is invisible but is still critical, like termites underground itching to nibble a wall.

The same need for maintenance is true for organizations and people. There is no final perfect condition. The environment changes. Objectives change. Things that were ok degrade. Who hasn't longed for an old team that had great chemistry and was highly productive? Who has not had some boss or mentor that was so supportive? These conditions are even more special because they do not last. We know even a great condition can worsen. A ship can start to get barnacles in just a few days. Hills that appear to be stable can shift and cover major roads in landslides. Instability is a constant. Untenable situations are particularly useful to look at because of their nature and seriousness. Stay diligent so that these situations are minimized, mitigated, or (ideally) nipped in the bud.

In conclusion, I would like to suggest these last points:

- Develop an ongoing sensitivity to unsustainable conditions that may sap your energy and hamper realization of your goals.
- Apply your creativity to solving problems and not for coming up with excuses or explanations.

- Don't think that people are always successful in all areas of their lives at the same time. Many successful people have untenable situations in various parts of their lives. It is healthy and natural to take these on to improve.
- Move with alacrity to tackle situations head-on.
- Get the issue out in the light of day and enlist trusted others to help.

…and lastly, have fun. Problems are evidence of life. Enjoy the process of solving them and creating a life you do enjoy.

It has been my great honor to share my thinking with you and I wish you every success.

About the Author

As a top executive coach and executive advisor, **Gary Covert** has worked with key leaders in some of the most admired companies around. These leaders are high-potential, critical decision-makers who work in complex, fast-paced environments with demanding stakeholders. The leaders who work with Gary regularly report improvements in profits, accelerated drive for results, and higher-functioning teams, as well as significant growth in individual and leadership effectiveness. Clients work in a diverse range of industries, including technology, global hospitality, eye health, restaurants and hospitality, health care, financial services, construction, defense, and energy.

Gary specializes in helping leaders reach their potential and boost their effectiveness. Any fool can be busy. Gary helps leaders build on their strengths to get more productive and have more fun doing it.

When he is not coaching leaders and their teams, you can find Gary in the gym, on a trail, playing with his dogs, or donating his expertise to worthy nonprofits.

Index

Accountability, 100
Adaptive actions, 87, 88
Alacrity, 94–95, 109
Aptitude, 106, 107
Aptitude to move, 4
Artificial intelligence, 39
Assertiveness, 71–74, 109
Assumption, 34
Augmented intelligence, 39–40
Authentic Happiness (Seligman), 81
Avoidance, 6–7
Awareness and action, 31–33

Back-seat barrier, 53–54
Bahrami, M., 56
Behaviors, 2–3
Being, roles of, 27
Belief, 34, 51
Big issues, 5
Blame, 55–57
Business, 87
    poor performer, 11
    successful, 24
    tackling, 85–88
Busting premises, 34–35
Busy, 34

Capacity, 7, 8
Care, 3
Career cost, 16–17
Coaching, 23
Coaching skills, 52, 56, 107
Collateral cost, 17–18
Compromise, 77
Consistent, 19
Contingent actions, 87
Continuous improvement, 110
Conviction, 106, 107
Conviction to move, 4
Cooper, B., 42
Corrective action, 87, 88
Cost, 3, 109

benefits, 19–20
career, 16–17
collateral, 17–18
context of health, 17
direct, 16
to dragging, 15–16
opportunity, 16
organizational, 17
surfacing, 20–21
Courage, fear and, 24–26
Critical issues, 65
Current state, 65

Direct costs, 16
Discipline, 106, 107
Discipline to move, 4

"Embrace the suck," 78
Emerging leader, 105
Enthusiasm, 46, 47, 94, 95
Environmental sources, 104
Excitement, 47

Fear, 64
    and courage, 24–26
Flexibility, 35

Game of Thrones, 78
Going kinetic, 92–94
Goldsmith, M., 9

Harrison, D., 79, 81, 95
Helpfulness, 79–83, 99–102
100 burpees, 66–68

Identity, 20
Impossibility thinking, 36–38

Jonah complex, 57–61

Kickoff point, 85
Kilmann, R., 77

Laziness, 20
Leaders, 28
    courageous, 26
    emerging, 105
    management practice, 25
    and organizations, 102–108
    senior, 106
Leadership, 3, 56, 105–104, 107
Leader–supervisor relationship, 56
Learned helplessness, 81
Learned Optimism (Seligman), 35
Lifestorming and *Thrive* (Weiss), 79

Making a stand, 78–79
Management, 25, 59, 60, 73, 78, 92,
    94
Managing, 60, 78, 80, 90
Maslow, A., 57–58, 60
Models, creating, 89–92
Momentum, 34

Negotiations, 35–36
The New Rational Manager (Kepner
    and Tregoe), 87

Objectification, 65
Obvious next step (ONS), 65
Opportunity cost, 16
Organizational calluses, 86
Organizational cost, 17
Organizational effectiveness, 1, 19
Organizations, 43, 107
    business and, 92
    dumb, 57
    glass ceilings, 59
    leaders and, 102–108
    maintenance, 110
    protection, 86
    untenable situations for, 108
Overcompensating effect, 29
Overplayed helpful, 79–83

Paradox Theory, 79
Performance growth cycle, 43
Perspective, 110

Possibility thinking, 109
Precursor, 54–55
Premises, 33–35
The Princess Bride, 61
Pro forma statements, 29–30

Quality, 23–24
Questions, 31–38

Ready stance, 73
Relationships, 20
Remembering, 72
Robo-calling, 87

Self-absorption, 81
Self-belief, 109
Self-reflective sources, 104
Self-trust, 51–52
Seligman, M., 35, 81
Senior leader, 106
Serious conditions, 10
Setting vision, 44–45
Slingshot effect, 29
Speed, 95
Standard keeping, 76, 77
Standards, 74–77
A Star Is Born (Cooper), 42
Success, 54, 56, 57, 89–90
Symptom, 28

Tackling business, 85–88
Team effectiveness, 28, 73
Teams, 48, 83
Thomas, K., 77
Tinkering, 85–87
Trailers (movie), 55
TV talent shows, 52

Uncertainty, 20
Underperformers, 8–9
Unsustainability, 9–10
Untenable situations, 1–8

Vicious cycles, 37–38
Visibility, vision, 45

Vision, 41–44, 47–48, 109
    discipline, 44–46
    and journey, 46–47
    untenable situation, 47
Vitality, vision, 45–46
Vulnerability, 110
    patches, 97–99

The Wall Street Journal, 47
Weiss, A., 79
Whale talk, 57–61
*What Got You Here Won't
    Get You There*
    (Goldsmith), 9
"Win-win" strategy, 72

OTHER TITLES IN THE HUMAN RESOURCE MANAGEMENT AND ORGANIZATIONAL BEHAVIOR COLLECTION

- *The Generation Myth* by Michael J. Urick
- *Practicing Leadership* by Alan S. Gutterman
- *Practicing Management* by Alan S. Gutterman
- *Women Leaders* by Sapna Welsh and Caroline Kersten
- *Comparative Management Studies* by Nelson E. Brestoff
- *Cross-Cultural Leadership Studies* by Richard M. Contino

Announcing the Business Expert Press Digital Library

Concise e-books business students need for classroom and research

This book can also be purchased in an e-book collection by your library as

- a one-time purchase,
- that is owned forever,
- allows for simultaneous readers,
- has no restrictions on printing, and
- can be downloaded as PDFs from within the library community.

Our digital library collections are a great solution to beat the rising cost of textbooks. E-books can be loaded into their course management systems or onto students' e-book readers.
The **Business Expert Press** digital libraries are very affordable, with no obligation to buy in future years. For more information, please visit **www.businessexpertpress.com/librarians**. To set up a trial in the United States, please email **sales@businessexpertpress.com**.

www.ingramcontent.com/pod-product-compliance
Lightning Source LLC
Chambersburg PA
CBHW052109230326
41599CB00054B/5196